EASY SPANISH

written and illustrated by **Shirley Herd**

for the:

**YACHTSMAN • FISHERMAN • RV'ER
AVIATOR • MOTORIST • TRAVELER**

S. DEAL & ASSOCIATES

San Diego

First printing: November, 1982
Second printing, revised: August, 1984
Third printing: September, 1989

Library of Congress Cataloging in
Publication Data

Herd, Shirley
    Easy Spanish for the yachtsman, RV'er, motorist, fisherman, aviator, traveler.
        Includes index.
    1. Spanish language—Conversation and phrase book.
    I. Title
    PC4121.H44 1982 468.3'421 82-17181
            ISBN: 0-930006-01-1

Published by:
S. Deal & Associates
1629 Guizot St.
San Diego, CA 92107

TABLE OF CONTENTS

OTHER BOOKS BY SHIRLEY HERD

  THE CRUISING COOK AND FIRST ADDITION
  BLIMEY, LIMEY! WHA'D HE SAY?

  Forthcoming titles by S. Deal & Associates:

    SAILING FOR PAY
    SECOND ADDITION TO THE CRUISING COOK

THANKS TO--

--Suzanne Herd Mencer, Spanish technical editor, who taught Spanish, grades 6-12 for nine years, and currently is employed by the U.S. Government as a Spanish linguist and specialist in Latin American Affairs. Affectionately known as "my sister Susie" throughout this book, she laboriously waded through, correcting accent marks, phonetic pronunciations and errors and adding constructive comments to all portions of the text...not to mention frequently voicing much needed encouragement to the author.

--D. J. Ryan, English editor of this text, Executive Director of the San Diego Apartment Association and editor of the "Rental Owners News" for the many weekends spent with her blue pencil attempting to right my 'wrongs.' And on occasion, emphatically stating "I want a disclaimer!" over certain grammatical nuances where the author had the final word.

--W. David Cookingham, Independent Marine Surveyor, Maritime Services Co., for his nautical and 'engines and tools' advice and, most of all, for moral support. Without his heartening comments, I would have thrown my 'toalla chica' in the ring, long before the book was completed.

--Jinny and Bob Ristau, neighbors, friends and knowledgeable aviators, for their time in reviewing and offering comments on the aviation chapter.

Because of each of you and your individual talents, **EASY SPANISH** is a better book.

Gracias.

Stomach fluttery? Palms damp? Is there an uncomfortable lump in your throat? Do you tingle with excitement then shudder with the fear of the unknown--or do both at the same time?

If so, you are suffering from a malady shared by millions of tourists annually:

The Before the Trip Grippe

1

I am delighted to say that few suffer long from this affliction; it's only temporary. Once you get across the border into that Spanish-speaking country, you will find those pre-trip anxieties melt away with the warmth of friendly smiles, people willing and wanting to help you, to make your visit to their country more enjoyable.

You won't be the first to misuse a verb tense, improperly use a word or incorrectly pronounce something. I've done it before you. But I'm not 'número uno.' Hordes of others have captured that First Place title ahead of me.

"Oh, sure, it's easy for you to tell me to stay calm," my girl friend mumbled, pacing the floor and wringing her hands. "After all, you were a Spanish teacher, you've got a solid background in Spanish. But I don't know a single word of Spanish."

If she only knew! Even with a knowledge of Spanish and with numerous trips abroad, I still make my share of errors.

Just to show you how easily it can happen to me, to you, to anyone...

THERE'S MANY A SLIP 'TWIXT THE CUP
AND THE LIP

-DE LA MANO A LA BOCA, SE PIERDE LA SOPA-

(or, loosely translated: from the hand to
the mouth, you can lose a lot of soup)

I was seated on an airplane next to a viva-
cious young woman from Germany who told me
how worried she was about her English.
Would she understand what the Californians
were saying?

I was truly amazed because her comprehen-
sion of and speaking abilities in English
were outstanding, better than some college
graduates I know. I assured her she
wouldn't have a problem. Why was she so
concerned?

"Well," she replied hesitantly, "I just
spent five days in New Orleans and I didn't
understand a word they said."

Can I sympathize with her feelings! I suffer not only in Louisiana but when listening to truckers on the CB while driving
across the heart of Dixie. Talk about a
foreign language!

Just as English varies from state to state,
so does Spanish. Even frequently used words
can differ from one Spanish-speaking country to another. In Mexico and Spain, a stop
sign says 'alto,' in Puerto Rico, it's
'pare.' A bus is an 'autobus' in these two
countries while in Puerto Rico, it's a
'guagua.'

The words I have selected for EASY SPANISH
will permit you to be understood--at least

3

8 out of 10 times. In some cases, several words are listed. If the first one you try doesn't light up the face of the other person, try the next. If you discover a word not included in this book, write it in for future use.

The pronunciations given are those used in most Spanish-speaking countries--the major exception is Spain. In Spain, Castilian Spanish is spoken. The difference is the pronunciation of the letter 'c' and 'z.' Instead of giving an 'ss' sound, it becomes a 'th' sound. For example, the word for maid or girl is 'moza.' It's generally pronounced 'MOH-sah' but in Spain, it becomes 'MOH-thah.'

A Spaniard will understand non-Castilian Spanish and because he is very proud of his "pure" language will try to teach it to you. And it's easy to learn. Although I had never been schooled in it, after a few days in Madrid, I was speaking almost like a native. I discovered the easy way: simply say any word with an 'ss' sound in it with a lisp--that's 'lithp' of course.

If I thought I was temporarily confused by the Spaniards' pronunciation, I was really baffled while in Puerto Rico--that is, until I realized what was happening. The Puerto Ricans tend to drop the last syllable of each word, especially, the 's' sound. Once I recognized their speech pattern, I could understand them.

As opposed to the Slavic languages with unfamiliar hard, guttural sounds, Spanish is one of the Romance languages with frequent similarities to English in spelling, translation, and pronunciation which makes

4

it easier for you to understand and speak: cigarro, diferente, falso, idea, cemento, telegrama are just a few examples.

But, be careful. Just because the word sounds or is spelled similarly does not always mean it's translated the same. I overheard a tourist exclaim, "Estoy embarazada," thinking she was saying how embarrassed she was. However, the Spanish verb 'embarazar,' colloquially, means to impregnate. I really don't think she meant to say she was pregnant.

The addition or omission of a single letter can change the meaning considerably. The verb 'casar' means married while the verb 'cansar' means tired. "Estoy cansada," I exclaimed when asked my marital status by an acquaintance from Villahermosa, Mexico-- who laughed and agreed I was probably right on both counts.

My sister Susie and I were seated at a table in Madrid, getting ready to order our first meal after arriving in Spain. I snapped my fingers, attempting to get the waiter's attention and boldly blurted out, "Camarón."

Susie looked shocked, shushed me and muttered, "Do you know what you just said?"

"Yes--well, I thought I did. I called the waiter."

"You called him all right. You called him 'shrimp.'

Thank heavens the waiter hadn't heard me. As you may know, many Spanish men are short: this waiter was a typical 5'6". I hadn't meant to call him a shrimp, I intended to say 'camarero.' But the similarities of words, mixed with a then rusty use of Spanish--I was truly embarrassed, in the deepest sense of the English meaning.

Sometimes gestures or words that are perfectly acceptable in the U.S. can take on unpleasant meanings in other countries. If you go to Mexico, avoid humming, singing or tapping a tune to "Shave and a haircut, two bits." The Mexican version of this translates into highly insulting street talk. The frequently used, innocuous (to us) gesture of forming a circle with the index finger and thumb, meaning 'ok' or 'looking good,' is an absolute no-no in many Latin American countries.

A stateside company adopted a handsome deer endowed with mystical and magical qualities as a corporate symbol. They mailed many important documents emblazoned with this seal to South America--only to find that in Brazil, the animal's name is street jargon for homosexual. An expensive error on their part.

Naturally, as a tourist in a foreign country, you cannot be expected to know about all things in advance and the people of that country will forgive and understand your lack of knowledge. Discovering these idiosyncracies, unique customs or traditions, first-hand, is more than half the fun of savoring a new country.

TIPS ABOUT

CLOTHING, CUSTOMS AND CONSIDERATIONS

Trying to observe another culture's customs or religious dogmas brings a great deal of respect from the natives. The predominant religion in most Spanish-speaking countries is Catholicism. In the past few years, the Catholic Church has changed many of its ways; however, I feel more comfortable visiting churches and cathedrals with a hat or scarf on my head although it is no longer required. In many countries, sleeveless blouses for women are not permitted in church. If I know I am going to be visiting a religious monument, I try to dress appropriately.

For women, the wearing of shorts in public is questionable. Wear a wrap-around skirt over them and remove it when you get to the beach. Although designer jeans are seen in the fanciest restaurants in the States, and even though I paid dearly for them, I will not wear them into restaurants for the customary, dressy evening meal when traveling abroad.

You'll be doing lots of sight-seeing so make sure you have a comfortable pair of shoes. I frequently wear sandals because they're the most comfortable walking shoes I own. During my first visit to Mexico City about 15 years ago, I couldn't imagine why people were staring at my feet. My thongs were new, and I thought, attractive--but not so appealing to warrant all those stares. I found out later the Mexicans were amazed that an American was so poor she couldn't afford shoes. At that time, only peasants wore sandals.

Whether you are going by land, sea or air, take a minimum, not maximum, of clothing. I have outfits that can be mixed and matched and take up only enough space to fill either one-half a suitcase or three-quarters of a duffel. Why only one bag and why not use all the available space? Number one, I detest managing more than one piece of luggage, but most important, I can use the empty portion of the container for souvenirs and trinkets. This method also acts as a buying check: when the bag gets full, it's time to quit shopping.

In addition to insect repellent and a sun screen lotion, a sun hat or cap is as practical as it is a necessity when you go to hot countries. If you don't want to carry a hat from home, put it on your list for first-day shopping. A Panama hat is cool and has one other distinct advantage: it can be successfully squashed into your pocket or purse and pops out fresh as a flower. In Puerto Vallarta, I found a Panama 'sombrero' for $12, a real bargain.

Customs in foreign countries are not only interesting but fun. Spain has a unique custom--the art of 'piropos.' Piropos are flattering compliments paid to pretty women as they walk by. Men from age 6 to 96 participate in this woman-watching-commenting national sport that should not be considered offensive.

By far the most exquisite use of piropos I heard was when Susie and I were in Arcos de la Frontera, a small town nestled high on a mountain between Sevilla and Cadiz. As we hiked by the church plaza, five gentlemen, ranging in age from 60 to 75, immaculately dressed in three-piece wool suits and black

8

wool berets were seated on benches in the full sun. Although the temperature was approaching 85 degrees, the heat did not wilt their desire to compliment. Practice through the years must make perfect and improve quality because not only were the comments of the highest order, they were all said in rhyme.

LIFE IN THE SLOW LANE

So many North Americans are used to life in the fast lane that when visiting a Spanish-speaking country where life has an overall slower pace, they have trouble adjusting to a 'mañana' attitude. When you get down to this concept, it's not a bad idea. After all, doubtlessly, you are there on vacation, not a business trip, so why not relax, lay back and appreciate your surroundings? If you accept the fact early on that anything you must accomplish will take longer than you ever imagined, you won't be frustrated or anxious. Recognize it as a new, temporary life style and enjoy it while you can. You'll be back to your mouse maze soon enough.

A 'siesta' is a custom to which I can easily adapt. These midday breaks can last from one hour to four hours or any combination in between. There doesn't seem to be any exact time schedule that's followed, just whatever is appropriate for that day. Stores can be closed anywhere from 11 a.m. to 4 p.m. so don't plan an impromptu shopping spree during these hours or you'll be disappointed that so few stores are open.

In Madrid, in the summer, this two to four hour break permits not only the working members of the family to come home but even the school children are dismissed. If you observe siesta, you'll discover that it's refreshing and sensible. It keeps you out of the exhausting heat of the day, gives you an opportunity to snuggle up with all those brochures you've collected and plan a tentative itinerary for the next day...with a stress on tentative. One of the keys to enjoying any vacation, especially one to the Land of Mañana, is to be flexible.

Because of this hearty meal and rest time, supper is served late. The dinner hour begins somewhere between 8 and 10 p.m. Your American time-tabled stomach may have trouble adjusting to its new feeding schedule, but it's only temporary.

PATIENCE PERSEVERES

Don't be afraid to try your Spanish no matter how inadequate you may feel it is. Seriously, you couldn't do worse than anyone else who is visiting. Even with the errors you are bound to make, if you try your bilingual tongue, you will find patient ears, friendly smiles and a willingness to understand and help you.

If you can't make yourself understood by speaking, don't hesitate to draw a picture or even use your hands to describe what it is you need. Sometimes this rudimentary form of communication will work--sometimes it won't.

During a motor home trip to mainland Mexico, I needed a funnel in order to properly fill the gasoline tank. The word for funnel was not in my conversational Spanish vocabulary--and, of course, my dictionary was reclining safely at home, gathering dust. I gestured to the attendant, describing the object with my hands while using words that were almost, but not quite, correct for what I wanted.

He smiled politely, nodding his head understandingly, then, turned and disappeared. I felt quite smug with my ability to communicate, to jury-rig, in the Spanish language and, quite obviously, be understood.

After fifteen minutes of tapping my toe, he reappeared and walked towards another customer's car with--you guessed it--a funnel.

I dashed over. "That's it! That's what I need," I blurted out in Spanish.

"Oh?" He seemed surprised I was still lingering about, that I needed something.

"Embudo?" he exclaimed in Spanish. "You wanted a funnel? Why didn't you say so!"

Even though on many occasions you, too, may 'lose a little soup' while communicating, you will indicate a willingness on your part to be accepted and be accepting of new ways and customs. And, believe me, if you do learn a new word through a personal experience, you won't forget it. 'Embudo' is firmly ensconced in my vocabulary.

The rules for maneuvering in any foreign country are the same: be friendly, polite, dress conservatively and you will be surprised how quickly the welcome door opens.

Most of all, communicate!

2/BASICS--BRIEFLY

(when all else fails, read this chapter)

If you're like most people, you breezed
through the introduction, read the chapter
on how to get across the border, then jump-
ed to the chapter that pertains to your
needs. What you saw probably seemed a bit
confusing--all that strange looking English. Now that you've returned to how to
interpret what you saw, let's begin.

As I mentioned earlier, many of the sounds in the English language are the same as Spanish--a few are different, such as those described in the consonant section of this chapter.

The vowels listed below, when written phonetically (as it is to be pronounced), appear as you see them--generally. For every rule, there's that you-can-count-on-it exception.

a = 'ah' in father

e = 'ay' in say or pay--when it ends
        a syllable; or, like
        'eh' in met--when followed by a
        consonant in the same syllable

i = 'ee' in reef, feet

o = 'oh' in row, slow

u = 'oo' in boot or food

y = 'ee' in feet, reef--you got it!
        The same as the 'i' sound.

Practice saying these vowels
                a = ah
                e = ay (or, eh)
                i = ee
                o = oh
                u = oo
until you can do it rapidly without thinking about it. Remember, this is how they will appear in the phonetic pronunciation.

DIPTHONGS

Dipthongs, in the simplest of terms, are two vowels, side-by-side. When placed in this position, a stress falls upon one of the two vowels. They are pronounced rapidly; don't dwell on either vowel. That is why in certain cases, you will see the two vowels phonetically represented as one. For example, 'ai' (AH-ee) becomes an 'eye' sound; 'au' (AH-oo) transforms to 'ow'; 'ue' is 'way'; 'ui' becomes 'we.'

When it is impossible to get a recognizable English word for a dipthong pronunciation because the result looks too weird to pronounce, you will find a mark (^) over the hyphen dividing the two vowels to remind you to say them as one. Stress the capitalized vowel if indicated.

In <u>EASY</u> <u>SPANISH</u>, I have eliminated any stumbling around or searching for the place to emphasize the word in order to pronounce it correctly. You will see where the accent or stress falls in each word because that group of words will always be CAPITALIZED.

CONSONANTS

Below are the consonants that are pronounced differently in Spanish than in English. Three are totally new sounds: ñ, r, and rr.

c = a soft sound like 'ss' if used before an 'e' or 'i'; sound, savor
    a hard 'k' sound otherwise; card, cord

g = a soft 'h' sound when it precedes 'e' or 'i'
    elsewhere, a hard sound; go, grin

h = NEVER pronounced

j = like an 'h'

ll = like 'y' in yet or yes

ñ = run together the phrase 'can yes' and the 'n-y' becomes an 'n-yeh' sound

qu = like 'k' in kay or key

r = is a bit tricky. Start by making the English 'r' sound, then flip your tongue against the roof of your mouth to make a trill sound--quickly. The best way to learn this one is to listen to a native say it.

rr = similar to the above 'r' but ex-aggerate the trill at the end

v = always like the English 'b'

x = similiar to an 'h' in English; or, like a 'ks' sound; exit

z = like 'ss' in sent or since

VERBS

Verbs, to me, are the most difficult part of the Spanish language so I had to make a decision: either delve into them deeply--or touch on them lightly. I chose the latter in order to make this text as simple as possible. You, as a traveler, basically need to know only the 'I' or 'we' form of the verb and because most of your needs are now, only the present, future or subjunc-tive tenses of verbs. Therefore, I elected to give you as many key phrases as possible that need only the infinitive after them. For example: 'I want' (key phrase) plus an 'infinitive' (to go, to buy, to see). The tedious chore of memorizing numerous verb changes and tenses is eliminated.

Take this system one step further and add nouns, adjectives or adverbs in the appropriate place to make a complete sentence:

```
I want......................Yoh kee-AIR-oh
  to buy..........................kohm-PRAHR
    a blue dress....oon behs-TEE-doh ah-sool
      and.................................ee
        cotton shirt...........kah-MEE-sah day
                      ahl-goh-DOHN.
```

(Yo quiero comprar un vestido azul y camisa de algodón.)

When it has been impossible to give you a key phrase, I have given you the total expression, phonetically and grammatically correct for instant speaking capabilities.

There is a major drawback to this method: it tends to limit conversational Spanish. However, if after your trip to the Spanish speaking country, you find you want to know more about the language and sharpen your skills, many fine text books and instructional classes are available that detail the intricacies of grammar. Because of your use and practice with this book, further study of the language will be easier.

AGREEMENT

The article 'the' that precedes a noun is usually 'el' for masculine words and 'la' for feminine. This is generally the rule, therefore, the article will not be shown in front of each word. For those words that violate this rule, the gender is indicated by an 'm' for masculine or 'f' for feminine just after the noun.

Adjectives also agree with the noun in gender and in a singular or plural form. Most masculine words end in 'o,' most feminine words end in 'a.' To form the plural add an 's' to either of these endings or 'es' if the word ends in a consonant.

The location of an adjective in the sentence depends upon what type of adjective it is. Non-descriptive adjectives (numerals, demonstratives, or indefinites) come before the subject. Descriptive adjectives normally follow the noun.

To say the fat lady in Spanish, you would say 'la mujer gorda.' Gorda, fat, is a descriptive adjective that follows the noun it modifies.

Another old man is 'otro hombre viejo.' The word 'otro' is an indefinite and 'viejo' describes the man.

Verb endings agree with the subject in a plural or singular form, and also change with the tense of the verb. Because of methods used in EASY SPANISH, you do not have to concern yourself with verbs.

PERSONAL PRONOUNS

Personal pronouns, I, we, you, etc., can clarify or emphasize the subject. They are:

```
I...................................yoh
          (yo)
you (singular)..................oos-TEHD
     (usted, abbreviated, ud.*)
he................................ehl
          (él)
```
*This abbreviation is used throughout this book.

```
she...............................AY-yah
           (ella)
it (rarely used).................AY-yoh
           (ello)
we................noh-SOH-trohs (-ahs)
        (nosotros, -ahs)
you (plural)...............oos-TEHD-ays
     (ustedes, abbreviated, uds.*)
they....................EH-yohs (-ahs)
          (ellos, -as)
```

Although all of this may sound a little
confusing right now, when you actually
start speaking the language, you will see
how it all fits together. And, as I mentioned earlier, if you boo-boo, you have an
accepting audience, eager to help you, to
teach you the right way.

At this point, you know all you need to
know about how to use <u>EASY SPANISH</u>. From
here on, the information is simply to help
you better understand the language or the
why's or how's of creating sentences. You
might wish to skim through the rest of this
chapter now--just to familiarize yourself
with its contents--then come back to it
after you've had an opportunity to test
your wings in Spanish.

*This abbreviation is used throughout
   this book.

OTHER GRAMMAR POINTS

To turn any positive statement into a negative, say 'no' preceding the verb.

To form an adverb from an adjective, add a '-mente' ending. 'Rápido' is 'rapidamente.'

To add a 'very small' meaning to a noun, adverb or adjective, use '-ito' or '-ita' at the end: 'ahora' is 'ahorita;' or say 'muy' in front of the word; 'muy poco.'

To show possession, John's book, is 'el libro de Juan' or literally, the book of John. The object the person possesses comes before the person and 'de' is used to indicate 'belonging to.'

'De' also is used to show 'made of.' In the example of the 'cotton shirt,' in Spanish, it would be 'la camisa de algodón.'

'Del' and 'al' are contractions formed by combining the words 'de el' or 'a el' which makes good sense because when you say the words quickly, that's the sound you get.

STRESS AND WRITTEN ACCENTS

If you're ever in doubt how a word should be pronounced, here's the rule:

In any combination using 'i' or 'y' or 'u' with any other vowel, the stress falls on the other vowel. When using 'i,' 'y' or 'u' together as a dipthong, the stress falls on the second vowel.

When encountering a word not in this dictionary, the stress rule is:

For words ending in 'n' or 's' or any vowel (except 'y') the stress falls on the next to last syllable. For other words, stress the last syllable. All words that violate these two rules have a written accent mark above the stressed syllable.

An accent mark (´) is used on a stressed 'i' or 'u' that would otherwise form a dipthong with the vowel next to it or to distinguish between two different words that sound alike but have another meaning.

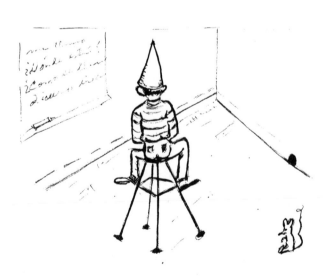

U.S.

MEXICO

Specific forms must be filled out <u>correctly</u> before entering Mexico and certain restrictions and regulations, both personal and legal, observed while you're there. U.S. Customs and Immigration also have a few requirements to meet before re-entering the States.

The first document required by Mexico of everyone, regardless of age, is a Tourist Card. The only exception is if you are planning to stay in Baja less than 72 hours. Without a tourist card, you may go as far south as San Felipe or along the other coast to Ensenada.

If a child is under 18 and not accompanied by the parents or with only one parent, the youngster needs a notarized affidavit stating he entered with the consent of his parents or guardian or, when applicable, the divorce papers or a death certificate. Either must be authenticated at a Mexican consulate.

TOURIST CARDS

Tourist cards are free and can be obtained from Mexican Immigration when you cross the border, any Mexican Consul or the Mexican National Tourist Council in larger U.S. cities and most travel agencies and airlines serving Mexico.

Tourist cards are good for up to 90 days but if the card is not used within 90 days of issuance, it expires. Stays of 180 days are authorized upon presentation of proof of economic solvency during a visit to Mexico.

To get a tourist card, you need a birth certificate, a voter's registration, a valid U.S. passport or a notarized affidavit as proof of U.S. citizenship. Citizens of other nations should consult the nearest Mexican Consulate regarding entry into Mexico.

The document presented as proof of citizenship should be carried into Mexico with the
tourist card. Photocopies of the documents
are not acceptable unless certified by the
issuing authority.

U.S. citizens transacting business of any
kind should inquire at the nearest Mexican
Consulate for detailed requirements. A
valid passport is usually required. Any
person traveling on business with only a
tourist card is subject to a fine.

FILLING OUT THE TOURIST CARD

Filling out the tourist card is easy because it's written in Spanish, French and
English. Simply print, in capitals, and
mark the appropriate boxes. The only items
you might not find are the signature lines.
Turn the form over and in the lower right
hand corner, in red, is a place for your
signature. Sign it. Now, open the document
and on the back side of page one, in blue
ink, is another signature line. Sign here,
too. You are now ready to cross the border.

MEXICAN LAW

The Mexican judicial system is based upon
Roman and Napoleonic law and therefore does
not assume the person is innocent until
proven guilty. There is no trial by jury
under this system. Guilt or innocence is
established by the prosecution and defense
counsel after examining documents on a
fixed date. This procedure is a long, drawn
out affair and although bail exists, it is
usually not granted to foreigners on the
premise they will leave Mexico. You do have
certain individual rights under the Mexican
Constitution but these rights are subject

to interpretation under Mexican judicial procedures that frequently differ significantly from our constitutional guarantees and judicial procedures. Americans in Mexico are subject to Mexican law, not U.S. law.

DRUGS

The trafficking and/or possession of drugs is a Federal offense and such cases are rigorously prosecuted. Because Mexican law does not differentiate between hard drugs, heroin, for example, and soft drugs, marijuana or amphetamines, all offenders are subject to the same prison sentences if found guilty: 7 to 15 years. Persons charged on drug violations are not eligible for release on bail during the trial process or for parole if found guilty. It is not uncommon for persons charged with drug offenses to be detained for periods up to one year before a verdict is reached.

Be wise, don't take drugs into Mexico.

GUNS

Hand guns are not permitted in Mexico. Shotguns are legal if accompanied by the properly filled-out form and a current letter from your local Police Department or Sheriff's Office stating that you have no criminal record. Two passport-sized photographs of good quality also are required. Be sure that Mexican custom officials check both the firearms and the permit authorizing their entry into the country.

REGISTERING ITEMS

If you plan to take foreign-made items such as cameras or binoculars with you, register them with U.S. Customs before crossing the border unless you possess the original receipts of purchase. This will avoid confusion when re-entering the U.S.

MEXICAN INSURANCE

Whether you are going to Mexico by motor vehicle, private plane or boat, you should consider purchasing Mexican insurance that will satisfy Mexico's Civil Responsibility Act for property damage or bodily injury caused to others.

Even though your American policy may give you limited coverage while you're in Mexico, such policies are not recognized by Mexico. Most states in Mexico require Mexican insurance. For more detailed information on insurance, see the beginning of each chapter that deals with your mode of traveling in Mexico: BOATS, CARS AND RV's or PLANES.

PETS

An American visiting Mexico may bring in a dog, cat or up to four canaries by presenting at the border:

1. A pet health certificate, Department of Agriculture, form 77-043, in duplicate, signed by a registered U.S. veterinarian. It must be issued no more than 72 hours before the animal enters Mexico.

2. A pet vaccination certificate showing that the animal has been treated for rabies, hepatitis, pip and leptospirosis.

Certification by Mexican consular authorities is not required for the health or vaccination certificate. A fee is charged at the time of entry into Mexico to issue the permit for the animal while it is in Mexico.

If the pet is out of the U.S. for more than 30 days, its owner must present the certificate when returning to the U.S.

SPECIAL PERMITS

Specific documents or permits are required if you enter Mexico by private plane, boat, motor vehicle or if you plan to fish. For detailed information about these forms, see the chapter that pertains to your needs; for example, at the beginning of BOATS, you will find the necessary information on yacht documentation.

HEALTH REQUIREMENTS

Vaccinations for smallpox are no longer necessary for entry into Mexico (or re-entry into the U.S.). However, before you leave the States, for your own peace of mind, make sure all those who are going have up-to-date shots. Get a vaccination or booster for tetanus or diptheria. If anyone in the family has missed the measles, mumps or polio vaccinations, get them, too. It may seem a bit irksome at the time but as stated by Dr. Myron G. Schultz, Center for Disease Control, "Americans tend to live sanitized lives and think other countries are just as sanitary. But that just isn't so. There are a lot of nasty 'bugs' out there just waiting to jump on you if you're careless."

TOURISTA - TRAVELER'S STOMACH

The most common affliction suffered by Americans abroad is probably the least serious. Known variously as "Montezuma's revenge" (Mexico), "Delhi belly" (India), the "Trotskys" (Russia) and in scientific circles, "traveler's diarrhea," it usually holds the unhappy tourist captive in his quarters for a miserable few days waiting for the disease--often linked to contaminated drinking water--to run its course.

Generally, when traveling in any nation where sanitary conditions may be suspect, it is safe to drink only hot beverages made with boiling water (such as tea or coffee), beer and wine, and canned or bottled carbonated water or beverages. Wipe the top dry, then drink straight from the container.

Beware of those tinkling, refreshing, cold ice cubes. They can be made from water that is not pure.

It is also wise to avoid unpasteurized milk and milk products (such as cheese), since they may cause intestinal problems or worse --they can harbor tuberculin bacteria.

Take along some medicine to prevent or ease traveler's diarrhea. If you are in doubt as to what medicine to buy, consult with your doctor.

Although I have never had a stomach problem during the 10 years I've been visiting

Baja, I can't say the same for mainland Mexico. Any produce that you buy, unless of course, you're cooking it, should be washed in water you know to be safe. Lettuce is the most difficult item to prepare because it grows close to the ground and irrigation water gets into the forming head. Each leaf needs to be carefully and individually washed before consuming. Although adding a few drops of chlorine to the rinse water speeds the deterioration of the lettuce, it will kill unwanted bacteria.

If you are eating in restaurants, be a bit leery of salads, tomatoes and the like: they may have been rinsed in contaminated water.

'COMFORT STATIONS'

Toilet facilities are as vital to individual survival as tourist cards are important to Mexican officials. Therefore, the words necessary to inquire where such accommodations are located are extremely valuable. You will find them at the end of this chapter, page 34.

Facilities won't have a Five Star rating so be prepared for most anything. Next to inoperative heads, the most common missing denominator is toilet paper. If you want to bring a roll from home, it will take less room in your luggage if you remove the cardboard holder and squash the roll flat. Take some with you in a purse or pocket for emergency situations.

EMERGENCY MEDICAL ASSISTANCE

Mexico has qualified doctors and good hospitals and medical facilities. However, if the situation is critical or if the patient would be more at ease back in the States, there is a company which specializes in just such care. Air-Evac, based in San Diego, will fly into any country where U.S. planes are permitted and fly the patient back to the closest hospital after crossing the border. If the situation is not critical, they will take the patient to his own hometown facilities.

In addition to the cockpit crew, are a qualified doctor and specialized nurse; for example, a Critical Case Registered Nurse, or if the patient is under 12 years of age, a pediatric nurse. The plane is equipped with modern medical equipment similar to a hospital's intensive care unit.

Air-Evac offers 24-hour service with a toll free 800 number. Several insurance programs are available and prices vary with the individual or family plan, how much coverage you desire, and where you plan to travel--Mexico, the Caribbean or Western Europe. If you live near a border town, such as San Diego or El Paso, and are traveling to Baja or nearby mainland Mexico, a small coverage policy of $10,000 is available and, perhaps, might be adequate. This individual plan costs $25 per year, a family plan, $38. A $20,000 plan is $45 per year for an individual and $68 for a family.

Even if you are not a client of Air-Evac's insurance programs, but require emergency medical treatment while abroad, they will still fly you back to the U.S. Estimated costs will be provided and financial arrangements made at the time of the evacuation.

For more information, write or call: Air-Evac International, Inc., 296 'H' St., Suite 301, Chula Vista, CA 92010. Phone: 800-854-2569 or (714) 425-4400.

IF YOU HAVE A PROBLEM

As a traveler, you should take common sense precautions to prevent thefts from happening. Lock your car or boat at all times, park your vehicle in well-lighted areas at night, keep valuables hidden from view (or don't take them with you in the first place), don't carry all your money in one purse, wallet or particularly, in your hip pocket.

In case of trouble, report immediately to the local police in major cities or to the 'delgado' in smaller towns. This elected official's duties include emergencies and civil or legal disputes. His office is at the Delegación Municipal or Sub-delegación.

In addition to the police, several other assisting agencies exist. One that you might not think about is the Department of Tourism. The very backbone of this government agency is to promote goodwill and develop tourism--you will find them extremely helpful. In Tijuana, Ensenada and Mexicali, the state government has a special office, Procuraduria de Protección al Turista (Attorney General for the Protection of Tourists), that acts as a public defender, consumer advocate and small claims court representative. Its services are free.

If your situation is serious--you lost your passport or you have insufficient funds to return home--as an American citizen, you should contact the U.S. Embassy or Consulate for assistance.

RETURNING TO THE U.S.

Each returning U.S. resident may bring back, duty-free, one liter of liquor per adult (21 years or older), and articles not exceeding $300 in retail value, providing they are for personal use and accompany the individual. If you have purchased some object that might appear to be more than this amount, even though you bartered and got it really cheap, you should have a receipt showing the amount actually paid. This $300 exemption may be used only once in a 31-day period.

The proof of citizenship presented to obtain a tourist card should be available to show U.S. Customs upon re-entering the U.S.

VOCABULARY

I have lost____...Hay pehr-DEE-doh mee____.
        (He perdido mi____.)
I have nothing to declare.
Noh TEHN-goh NAH-dah PAH-rah day-klah-RAHR.
        (No tengo nada para declarar.)

address..................dee-rehk-see‑OHN
                (dirección, f)
age...............................ay-DAHD
                (edad, f)
American.................ah-may-ree-KAH-noh
                (americano, -a)
American Consul
        ....KOHN-sool ah-may-ree-KAH-noh
                (cónsul americano)
Attorney General for the Protection of
   Tourists
        ....proh-koo-rah-doo-REE‑ah day
        proh-tehk-see‑OHN ahl too-REES-tah
        (Procuraduría de Protección al Turista)
border..........................BORH-doh
                (bordo)
   or.........................LEE-nay‑ah
                (línea)
city.........................see‑oo-DAHD
                (ciudad, f)
clearance.....days-PAH-choh day ah-DWAH-nah
                (despacho de aduana)
customs.......................ah-DWAH-nah
                (aduana)
delgado.......................dehl-GAH-doh
Delegación Municipal
   ....day-lay-gah-see‑OHN moo-nee-see-PAHL
   Sub-delegación
   ....soob day-lay-gah-see‑OHN
Department of Tourism
   ..day-pahr-tah-MEHN-toh day too-REES-moh
        (departamento de turismo)
document...................doh-koo-MEHN-toh
                (documento)

32

driver's license
........lee-SEHN-see^ah day mah-nay-HAHR
          (licencia de manejar)
embassy....................ehm-bah-HAH-dah
              (embajada)
immigration............een-mee-grah-see^OHN
              (inmigración)
   or.....................mee-grah-see^OHN
              (migración)
marital status.........ehs-TAH-doh see-BEEL
              (estado civil)
   divorced.............dee-bohr-see^AH-doh
              (divorciado, -a)
   married.....................kah-SAH-doh
              (casado, -a)
   single......................sohl-TAY-roh
              (soltero, -a)
   widowed.....................bee^OO-doh
              (viudo, -a)
name............................NOHM-bray
              (nombre, m)
   last name................ah-pay-YEE-doh
              (apellido)
nationality.........nah-see^oh-nah-lee-DAHD
              (nacionalidad, f)
occupation..............oh-koo-pah-see^OHN
              (ocupación, f)
passport...................pah-sah-POHR-tay
              (pasaporte, m)
police......................poh-lee-SEE^ah
              (policía)
   police station.......koh-mee-SAH-ree^oh
              (comisario)
port captain.............kah-pee-tah-NEE^ah
              (capitanía)
profession................proh-fay-see^OHN
              (profesión, f)
quarantine...............kwah-rehn-TAY-nah
              (cuarentena)
signature.........................FEER-mah
              (firma)

```
state........................ehs-TAH-doh
              (estado)
tourist card..tahr-HAY-tah day too-REES-tah
          (tarjeta de turista)
vaccination card
    ....sehr-tee-fee-KAH-doh day bah-KOO-nah
          (certificado de vacuna)
```

COMFORT FACILITIES

```
Where is the bathroom?
    .................¿DOHN-day ehs-TAH____?
          (¿Dónde está____?)
    .................lohs sehr-BEE-see^ohs
          (los servicios)
    ......................ehl ray-TRAH-toh
          (el retrato)
    ....................ehl ehs-koo-SAH-doh
          (el escusado)
    ...........lohs kah-bah-YAY-rohs (men)
          (los caballeros)
    ................lahs DAH-mahs (women)
          (las damas)
    ........................ehl BAH-nyoh
          (el baño)
    note:  BAH-nyohs--baños--are bath houses

I need____............Nay-say-see-toh____.
          (Necesito____.)
    soap.........................hah-BOHN
          (jabón, m)
    toilet paper..pah-PEHL ee-hee^EH-nee-koh
          (papel higiénico)
       or.............pah-PEHL day BAH-nyoh
          (papel de baño)
    paper towels.....toh^AH-yahs de pah-PEHL
          (toallas de papel)
```

¡Ole! You are across the border and on your way! This chapter, loaded with important key words and phrases of a general nature, will be the one you refer to most--and want to learn thoroughly.

If you are looking for specific vocabulary words, such as for hotels, tools, transportation, or food, turn to the section that deals with that subject. Frequently, you will find the fundamental expression in this chapter repeated in the others--for your convenience.

NUMBERS

Memorize numbers. You will be using them daily--for buying items, paying a cabbie, telling time and so on. They are not difficult to remember and are well worth the time required to learn them well.

```
numbers......................NOO-may-rohs
            (números)
1.................................OO-noh
            (uno)
2...................................dohs
            (dos)
3..................................trehs
            (tres)
4.............................KWAH-troh
            (cuatro)
5.............................SEEN-koh
            (cinco)
6...................................sehs
            (seis)
7..........................see‿AY-tay
            (siete)
8.............................OH-choh
            (ocho)
9.............................NWAY-bay
            (nueve)
10..........................dee‿EHS
            (diez)
11...........................OHN-say
            (once)
12...........................DOH-say
            (doce)
13...........................TRAY-say
            (trece)
14........................kah-TOHR-say
            (catorce)
15...........................KEEN-say
            (quince)
```

After 15, counting is a combination of numbers: 16 is, literally, 10 and 6 (diez y seis or can be written diesiséis), 37 is thirty and seven (treinta y siete), etc.

```
16..........................dee-ehs-ee-SEHS
            (diesiséis)
17...................dee-ehs-ee-see-AY-tay
            (diesisiete)
18......................dee-ehs-ee-OH-choh
            (diesiocho)
19...................dee-ehs-ee-noo-AY-bay
            (diesinueve)
20................................BEHN-tay
            (veinte)
30...............................TREHN-tah
            (treinta)
40...........................kwah-REHN-tah
            (cuarenta)
50...........................seen-KWEHN-tah
            (cincuenta)
60...........................say-SEHN-tah
            (sesenta)
70...........................say-TEHN-tah
            (setenta)
80............................oh-CHEN-tah
            (ochenta)
90...........................noh-BEHN-tah
            (noventa)
100..............................see-EHN
            (cien)
200.....................dohs see-EHN-tohs
            (dos cientos)
300.....................trehs see-EHN-tohs
            (tres cientos)
400................KWAH-troh see-EHN-tohs
            (cuatro cientos)
500.....................kee-nee-EHN-tohs
            (quienientos)
1000................................meel
            (mil)
```

```
10,000........................dee-EHS meel
             (diez mil)
100,000.......................see-EHN meel
             (cien mil)
million..........................mee-YOHN
             (millón)
billion..........................bee-YOHN
             (billón)
```

ORDINAL NUMBERS

```
first...........................pree-MAY-roh
             (primero)
second..........................say-GOON-doh
             (segundo)
third...........................tehr-SAY-roh
             (tercero)
fourth..........................KWAHR-toh
             (cuarto)
fifth...........................KEEN-toh
             (quinto)
sixth...........................SEKS-toh
             (sexto)
seventh.........................SEHP-tee-moh
             (séptimo)
eighth..........................ohk-TAH-boh
             (octavo)
ninth...........................noh-BAY-noh
             (noveno)
tenth...........................DAY-see-moh
             (décimo)
```

TELLING TIME

Now that you have learned your numbers,
telling time will be a snap--well, almost.

In telling time, hour (hora) is used and
the article and verb agree with <u>hora</u> or
<u>horas</u> which is understood but not said
except when you say...

What time is it?...........¿Kay OH-rah ehs?
(¿Qué hora es?)

The singular form of the verb <u>ser</u> is used with one o'clock and the plural is used for all other hours.

It is one o'clock............Ehs lah OO-nah.
(Es la una.)

It is two o'clock...........Sohn lahs dohs.
(Son las dos.)

Fifteen, <u>cuarto</u>, is used as quarter-past or quarter-to the hour and <u>media</u> for half-past the hour.

It is quarter-past three.
...........Sohn lahs trehs ee KWAHR-toh.
(Son las tres y cuarto.)

It is half-past four (four-thirty).
......Sohn lahs KWAH-troh ee MAY-dee~ah.
(Son las cuatro y media.)

Time past the hour is preceded by y or con
and before the hour by menos or para.

It is three-twenty.
.........Sohn lahs trehs kohn BAYN-tay.
(Son las tres con veinte.)

It is quarter to one.
......Ehs lah OO-nah MAY-nohs KWAHR-toh.
(Es la una menos cuarto.)

Phrases beginning with the preposition de
are used if the hour is stated, or, if it
merely indicates a.m or p.m., with a phrase
starting with por.

It is four in the afternoon.
...Sohn lahs KWAH-troh day lah TAHR-day.
(Son las cuatro de la tarde.)

I am going to town in the morning.
Boy ahl SEHN-troh pohr lah mah-NYAH-nah.
(Voy al centro por la mañana.)

VOCABULARY

afternoon.........................TAHR-day
            (tarde, f)
before dark...............ah-noh-chay-SEHR
            (anochecer, m)
day...............................DEE-ah
            (día, m)
early....................tehm-PRAH-noh
            (temprano)

40

```
exactly on the hour...........ehn POON-toh
              (en punto)
future.......................foo-TOO-roh
              (futuro)
half hour....................MAY-dee-ah
              (media)
hour.........................OH-rah
              (hora)
in the afternoon.........pohr lah TAHR-day
              (por la tarde)
in the evening...........pohr lah NOH-chay
              (por la noche)
in the morning.......pohr la mah-NYAH-nah
              (por la mañana)
last night...................ah-NOH-chay
              (anoche)
last year..........ehl AH-nyoh pah-SAH-doh
              (el año pasado)
late.........................TAHR-day
              (tarde)
midnight..............MAY-dee-ah-NOH-chay
              (medianoche)
minute.......................mee-NOO-toh
              (minuto)
night........................NOH-chay
              (noche, f)
noon..................MAY-dee-ah-DEE-ah
              (mediadía, m)
quarter to...................KWAHR-toh
              (cuarto)
second.......................say-GOON-doh
              (segundo)
today........................OH-ee
              (hoy)
tomorrow.....................mah-NYAH-nah
              (mañana)
tonight.................EHS-tah NOH-chay
              (esta noche)
year.........................AH-nyoh
              (año)
yesterday....................ah-YEHR
              (ayer)
```

41

DAYS OF THE WEEK

week.............................say-MAH-nah
                (semana)
Monday...........................LOO-nays
                (lunes)
Tuesday..........................MAHR-tays
                (martes)
Wednesday.................mee͜EHR-koh-lays
                (miércoles)
Thursday.........................HWAY-bays
                (jueves)
Friday.......................bee͜EHR-nays
                (viernes)
Saturday.....................SAH-bah-doh
                (sábado)
Sunday.......................doh-MEEN-goh
                (domingo)

MONTHS

months...........................MAY-sehs
                (meses, m)
January......................ay-NAY-roh
                (enero)
February....................fay-BRAY-roh
                (febrero)
March............................MAHR-soh
                (marzo)
April............................ah-BREEL
                (abril)
May..............................MAH-yoh
                (mayo)
June.........................HOO-nee͜oh
                (junio)
July.........................HOO-lee͜oh
                (julio)
August.......................ah-GOHS-toh
                (agosto)
September................sehp-tee͜EHM-bray
                (septiembre)

42

October.......................ohk-TOO-bray
                (octubre)
November..................noh-bee^EHM-bray
                (noviembre)
December..................dee-see^EHM-bray
                (diciembre)

SEASONS

seasons.................ehs-tah-see^OHN-ays
            (estaciones, m)
autumn........................oh-TOH-nyoh
                (otoño)
spring....................pree-mah-BAY-rah
                (primavera)
summer........................bay-RAH-noh
                (verano)
winter....................een-bee^EHR-noh
                (invierno)

COLORS

colors........................koh-LOH-rays
                (colores, m)
amber............................AHM-bahr
                (ámbar)
black............................NAY-groh
                (negro)
blue.............................ah-SOOL
                (azul)
brown............................kah-FAY
                (café)
gold.............................OH-roh
                (oro)
grey...............................grees
                (gris)
green...........................BEHR-day
                (verde)
orange.................ah-nah-rahn-HAH-doh
                (anaranjado)
pink.............................ROH-sah
                (rosa)

43

```
purple.....................bee-oh-LAY-tah
                (violeta)
red........................ROH-hoh
                (rojo)
silver.....................PLAH-tah
                (plata)
white......................BLAHN-koh
                (blanco)
yellow.....................ah-mah-REE-yoh
                (amarillo)
```

GREETINGS

```
hello......................OH-lah
                (hola)
good bye...................ah-dee-OHS
                (adiós)
good morning (until noon)
.....................BWAY-nohs DEE-ahs
            (buenos días)
good afternoon (noon to sunset)
.....................BWAY-nahs TAHR-days
            (buenas tardes)
good night.............BWAY-nahs NOH-chays
                (buenas noches)
What is your name?
.........¿KOH-moh say YAH-mah oos-TEHD?
          (¿Cómo se llama ud?)
My name is____...........May YAH-moh____.
          (Me llamo____.)
I am happy to meet you.
    MOO-choh GOOS-toh ehn koh-noh-SEHR-lay.
        (Mucho gusto en conocerle.)
The pleasure is mine.
...............Ehl GOOS-toh ehs MEE-oh.
          (El gusto es mío.)
At your service.......Ah soos OHR-day-nays.
                (A sus órdenes.)
How are you?.....¿KOH-moh ehs-TAH oos-TEHD?
                (¿Cómo está ud.?)
```

44

```
Very well, thank you. And you?
MOO^ee bee^EHN, GRAH-see^ahs. ¿Ee oos-TEHD?
        (Muy bien, gracias. ¿Y ud.?)
What is the matter?...........¿Kay PAH-sah?
                (¿Qué pasa?)
What happened?................¿Kay pah-SOH?
                (¿Qué pasó?)
I think so................KRAY-oh kay see.
                (Creo que sí.)
I do not think so.........Noh loh KRAY-oh.
                (No lo creo.)
please......................pohr fah-BOHR
                (por favor)
thank you....................GRAH-see^ahs
                (gracias)
See you later...........AHS-tah loo^AY-goh.
                (Hasta luego.)
See you tomorrow......AHS-tah mah-NYAH-nah.
                (Hasta mañana.)
How goes it?....................¿Kay tahl?
                (¿Qué tal?)
Good luck!.............¡BWAY-nah SWEHR-tay!
                (¡Buena suerte!)
With your permission.Kohn soo pehr-MEE-soh.
                (Con su permiso.)
Hey!................................¡OH-yay!
                (¡Oye!)
Hey!............................s-s-s-s-s
        (a common sound to get attention)
```

KEY EXPRESSIONS

These expressions only need to be followed
by a verb in the infinitive form--to buy,
to go, to see. Numerous verbs in this state
are found, beginning on page 52.

```
I need____ .............Nay-say-SEE-toh____ .
                (Necesito____ .)
   We need____ ......Nay-say-see-TAH-mohs__ .
        (Necesitamos____ .)
```

45

```
I want_____ ...................Kee-AIR-oh____.
              (Quiero____.)
   We want_____ ...........Kay-RAY-mohs____.
              (Queremos____.)
I like_____ ...............May GOOS-tah____.
              (Me gusta____.)
   We like_____ ...........Nohs GOOS-tah____.
              (Nos gusta____.)
I would like_____ ........Kee-see-AY-rah____.
              (Quisiera____.)
   We would like_____ ...Kee-see-AY-rah-mos___.
              (Quisiéramos____.)
```

A useful, popular expression used to mean:
"There is or there are____" ....Eye____.
              (Hay____.)

This same expression, used with a negative,
means many things; "there is not one, there
are not any, all gone, we do not carry any
or we do not have any": ....Noh eye.
              (No hay.)

Another popular expression that means some-
thing does not work: ....Noh SEER-bay.
              (No sirve.)
It is broken ....Say kay-BROH.
              (Se quebró.)
It needs_____ ....Say nay-say-SEE-tah____.
        (Se necesita____.)
_____ is necessary.
  ....Ehs nay-say-SAHR-ee-oh____.
              (Es necesario____.)

If you do not understand the reply, say one
of the following:
I do not understand.....Noh kohm-PREHN-doh.
              (No comprendo.)
   or ....MAHN-day.
              (Mande.)
  (which literally means, send whatever you
  said again.)

                    46

I do not speak Spanish well.....Noh AH-bloh
    MOO⌢ee bee⌢EHN ehl ehs-pah-NYOHL.
        (No hablo muy bien el español.)
Repeat, please.
        ....Ray-PEE-tah, pohr fah-BOHR.
                (Repita, por favor.)
Speak more slowly.
        ....HAH-blay mahs days-PAH-see⌢oh.
                (Hable más despacio.)
What are you saying?..¿KOH-moh say DEE-say?
                (¿Cómo se dice?)
Do you speak English?...¿AH-blah een-GLAYS?
                (¿Habla inglés?)
Who speaks English?
        ....¿Kee⌢EHN AH-blah een-GLAYS?
            (¿Quién habla inglés?)
I need an interpreter.
        ..Nay-say-SEE-toh oon een-TEHR-pray-tay.
            (Necesito un intérprete.)
Do you understand me?
        ....¿May ehn-tee⌢EHN-day oos-TEHD?
                (¿Me entiende ud.?)

KEY QUESTIONS

How do you say____in Spanish?
¿KOH-moh say DEE-say____ehn ehs-pah-NYOHL?
        (¿Cómo se dice____en español?)
What is this called?
        ....¿KOH-moh say YAH-mah?
                (¿Cómo se llama?)
Do you have____?
        ....¿Tee⌢AY-nay oos-TEHD____.
                (¿Tiene ud.____?.
Do they have____?
        ....¿Tee⌢AY-nehn oos-TEHD-ays____.
                (¿Tienen uds.____?)
Can you help me?
        .....¿PWAY-day oos-TEHD ah-yoo-DAHR-may?
            (¿Puede ud. ayudarme?)
Is it possible____?..¿Ehs poh-SEE-blay____.
                (¿Es posible____?)

```
How much is this?........¿KWAHN-toh BAH-lay?
              (¿Cuánto vale?)
   or................¿KWAHN-toh KWEHS-tah?
              (¿Cuánto cuesta?)
Where is (location)?
   ................¿DOHN-day ehs-TAH___?
         (¿Dónde está___?)
How many___?..............¿KWAHN-tohs___?
         (¿Cuántos___?)
Where can I buy___?
   ...¿DOHN-day say PWAY-day kohm-PRAHR___?
     (¿Dónde se puede comprar___?)
Do you know (a person)?
   ...................¿Koh-NOH-say ah___?
         (¿Conoce a___?)
Do you know (a fact or thing)?
   .........................¿SAH-bay___?
         (¿Sabe___?)
Can you fix___?
   ....¿PWAY-day oos-TEHD ray-pah-RAHR___?
       (¿Puede ud. reparar___?)
Who?.........................¿Kee-EHN?
         (¿Quién?)
Who is___?..............¿Kee-EHN ehs___?
         (¿Quién es___?)
What?.........................¿Kay?
         (¿Qué?)
What is this?............¿Kay ehs EHS-tah?
         (¿Qué es ésta?)
When?.....................¿KWAHN-doh?
         (¿Cuándo?)
Where?.....................¿DOHN-day?
         (¿Dónde?)
Why?..........................¿Pohr kay?
         (¿Por qué?)
How much?..................¿KWAHN-toh?
         (¿Cuánto?)
```

Expressions with the verb TENER

The verb tener is to have but when used
with the following words it means:

I am____ ....TEHN-goh____.
                  (Tengo)

    warm.......................kah-LOHR
                 (calor)

    cold.......................FREE⌃oh
                 (frío)

    hungry.....................AHM-bray
                 (hambre)

    thirsty........................sehd
                 (sed)

    sleepy....................SWAY-nyoh
                 (sueño)

    afraid...................mee⌃AY-doh
                 (miedo)

    right.....................rah-SOHN
                 (razón)

    twenty years old...BEHN-tay AH-nyohs
          (veinte años.)
           (How I wish!)

    in a hurry..................PREE-sah
                 (prisa)

Besides those expressions with tener, there
are two other forms that are helpful:

Use tengo followed by ganas de then the
infinitive to express I feel like. To indicate we, say tenemos and then the rest of
the expression. Insert any verb--that
makes sense, of course--in its infinitive
form to express your desires with this
useful phrase.

I feel like_____ (going out).
TEHN-goh GAH-nahs day____(sah-LEER).
(Tengo ganas de salir.)
We feel like____..........Tay-NAY-mohs____.
(Tenemos____.)

Another helpful expression that means to have to is formed by using que after tengo or tenemos or any form of tener:

I have to study alot.
TEHN-goh kay ehs-too-dee^AHR MOO-choh.
(Tengo que estudiar mucho.)

MORE EXPRESSIONS OR WORDS

again..........................OH-trah behs
(otra vez)
as if..........................KOH-moh see
(como si)
as soon as....................ehn KWAHN-toh
(en cuanto)
at last..........................pohr feen
(por fin)
because..........................pohr-KAY
(porque)
everybody.............TOH-doh ehl MOON-doh
(todo el mundo)
everything..........................TOH-doh
(todo)
everywhere.........pohr TOH-dahs PAHR-tehs
(por todas partes)
immediately................ehn say-GEE-dah
(en seguida)
It is all right...........Ehs-TAH bee^EHN.
(Está bien.)
little by little.........POH-koh ah POH-koh
(poco a poco)
nevertheless.............seen ehm-BARH-goh
(sin embargo)
of course.......................KOH-moh noh
(cómo no)

only..........................noh mahs kay
        (no más que)
..........................soh-lah-MEHN-tay
        (solamente)
so...............................ah-SEE
        (así)
so so........................ah-SEE ah-SEE
        (así así)
some.........................ahl-GOO-noh
        (alguno)
  or.............................OO-nohs
        (unos)
someone......................ahl-gee-EHN
        (alguien)
something.........................AHL-goh
        (algo)
somewhere.........ehn ahl-GOO-nah PAHR-tay
        (en alguna parte)
soon............................PROHN-toh
        (pronto)
suddenly....................day PROHN-toh
        (de pronto)
that is right...................EH-soh ehs
        (eso es)
these......................EHS-tohs (-ahs)
        (estos, estas)
this.......................EHS-tay (-ah)
        (este, esta)
those.........EH-sohs (-sahs), ah-KAY-yohs
        (esos, esas, aquellos)
too...........................tahm-bee-EHN
        (también)
too much................day-mah-see-AH-doh
        (demasiado)
very.............................MOO-ee
        (muy)
What a pity!.............¡Kay LAHS-tee-mah!
        (¡Qué lástima!)
To your health!...........¡Ah soo sah-LOOD!
        (¡A su salud!)

VERBS FOR EVERYONE

TO:

allow..............................day-HAHR
                  (dejar)
answer........................kohn-tehs-TAHR
                  (constestar)
arrive.............................yay-GAHR
                  (llegar)
ask...........................pray-goon-TAHR
                  (preguntar)
awaken.......................days-pehr-TAHR
                  (despertar)
be (state of permanency)..............sehr
                  (ser)
   (state of change)...............ehs-TAHR
                  (estar)
begin.......................ehm-pay-SAHR
                  (empezar)
believe..........................kray‑EHR
                  (creer)
bet..........................ah-pohs-TAHR
                  (apostar)
break.............................rohm-PEHR
                  (romper)
bring............................trah‑EHR
                  (traer)
buy..............................kohm-PRAHR
                  (comprar)
call............................yah-MAHR
                  (llamar)
carry............................yay-BAHR
                  (llevar)
change or exchange............kahm-bee‑AHR
                  (cambiar)
close, shut.....................say-RRAHR
                  (cerrar)
come............................bay-NEER
                  (venir)
come back, return................bohl-BEHR
                  (volver)

52

```
consider................kohn-see-day-RAHR
            (considerar)
continue, follow.................say-GEER
            (seguir)
cross..........................kroo-SAHR
            (cruzar)
decide.....................ray-sohl-BEHR
            (resolver)
die...........................moh-REER
            (morir)
discover...................dehs-koo-BREER
            (descubrir)
dive..........................klah-BAHR
            (clavar)
   as skin dive..............boo-say^AHR
            (bucear)
do.............................ah-SEHR
            (hacer)
dress.........................behs-TEER
            (vestir)
drink.........................toh-MAHR
            (tomar)
   or.........................bay-BEHR
            (beber)
drive......................mah-nay-HAHR
            (manejar)
eat...........................koh-MEHR
            (comer)
empty.......................bah-see^AHR
            (vaciar)
enter.........................ehn-TRAHR
            (entrar)
explain....................eks-plee-KAHR
            (explicar)
fight........................pay-lay^AHR
            (pelear)
fill..........................yay-NAHR
            (llenar)
find...........................ah-YAHR
            (hallar)
finish.....................tehr-mee-NAHR
            (terminar)
```

```
fish...............................pehs-KAHR
                (pescar)
fix................................ah-rray-GLAHR
                (arreglar)
forget.............................ohl-bee-DAHR
                (olvidar)
forgive............................pehr-doh-NAHR
                (perdonar)
get................................ohb-tay-NEHR
                (obtener)
give...............................dahr
                (dar)
go.................................eer
                (ir)
go away............................EER-say
                (irse)
have...............................tay-NEHR
                (tener)
help...............................ah-yoo-DAHR
                (ayudar)
hunt...............................kah-SAHR
                (cazar)
import.............................eem-pohr-TAHR
                (importar)
insure.............................ah-say-goo-RAHR
                (asegurar)
introduce..........................pray-sehn-TAHR
                (presentar)
invite.............................een-bee-TAHR
                (invitar)
keep...............................gwahr-DAHR
                (guardar)
know (how or facts)................sah-BEHR
                (saber)
    (a person)....................koh-noh-SEHR
                (conocer)
learn..............................ah-prehn-DEHR
                (aprender)
leave..............................sah-LEER
                (salir)
lend or loan.......................prehs-TAHR
                (prestar)
```

```
like..........................goos-TAHR
              (gustar)
listen.....................ehs-koo-CHAHR
              (escuchar)
live..........................bee-BEER
              (vivir)
look at.......................mee-RAHR
              (mirar)
look for......................boos-KAHR
              (buscar)
lose..........................pehr-DEHR
              (perder)
love..........................kay-REHR
              (querer)
lower.........................bah-HAHR
              (bajar)
make..........................ah-SEHR
              (hacer)
meet......................ehn-kohn-TRAHR
              (encontrar)
must (ought)..................day-BEHR
              (deber)
name..........................yah-MAHR
              (llamar)
navigate...................nah-bay-GAHR
              (navegar)
need.....................nay-say-see-TAHR
              (necesitar)
obtain.....................ohb-tay-NEHR
              (obtener)
occupy.....................oh-koo-PAHR
              (ocupar)
offer......................oh-fray-SEHR
              (ofrecer)
open..........................ah-BREER
              (abrir)
order......................ohr-day-NAHR
              (ordenar)
 or...........................mahn-DAHR
              (mandar)
owe...........................day-BEHR
              (deber)
```

```
pay.............................pah-GAHR
                (pagar)
pay attention...................fee-HAHR
                (fijar)
permit......................pehr-mee-TEER
                (permitir)
play............................hoo-GAHR
                (jugar)
prohibit....................pro-hee-BEER
                (prohibir)
put............................poh-NEHR
                (poner)
put in.........................may-TEHR
                (meter)
raise......................lay-bahn-TAHR
                (levantar)
reach..........................yay-GAHR
                (llegar)
read...........................lay-EHR
                (leer)
remember...................ray-kohr-DAHR
                (recordar)
remove.....................ray-moh-BEHR
                (remover)
rent...........................rehn-TAHR
                (rentar)
    or.....................ahl-kee-LAHR
                (alquilar)
repair.....................ray-pah-RAHR
                (reparar)
    or.....................ah-rray-GLAHR
                (arreglar)
repeat.....................ray-pay-TEER
                (repetir)
reply......................kohn-tehs-TAHR
                (contestar)
request........................pay-DEER
                (pedir)
return.........................bohl-BEHR
                (volver)
run...........................koh-RREHR
                (correr)
```

```
say.................................day-SEER
                (decir)
see...................................behr
                (ver)
sell...........................behn-DEHR
                (vender)
send........................mahn-DAHR
                (mandar)
shave.....................rah-soo-RAHR
                (rasurar)
sign..........................feer-MAHR
                (firmar)
sleep........................dohr-MEER
                (dormir)
solve.....................ray-sohl-BEHR
                (resolver)
sorry (to be or feel)............sehn-TEER
                (sentir)
speak..........................ah-BLAHR
                (hablar)
spend........................gahs-TAHR
                (gastar)
start (like a car)...........ah-rrahn-KAHR
                (arrancar)
     (like a job)............koh-mehn-SAHR
                (comenzar)
stay...........................kay-DAHR
                (quedar)
stop..........................pah-RAHR
                (parar)
study.....................ehs-too-dee-AHR
                (estudiar)
swim.........................nah-DAHR
                (nadar)
take (a trip)........ah-SEHR oon bee-AH-hay
            (hacer un viaje)
take (carry)......................yay-BAHR
                (llevar)
take apart..................day-sahr-MAHR
                (desarmar)
take out..........................sah-KAHR
                (sacar)
```

57

```
talk.............................ah-BLAHR
                (hablar)
teach......................ehn-say-NYAHR
                (enseñar)
telephone..............tay-lay-foh-nay-AHR
                (telefonear)
tell.............................day-SEER
                (decir)
think (about)..............pehn-SAHR (ehn)
                (pensar en)
tie (as knots).................ah-mah-RRAHR
                (amarrar)
travel.......................bee-ah-HAHR
                (viajar)
turn off (as lights)............ah-pah-GAHR
                (apagar)
        (as water)...............sehr-RAHR
                (cerrar)
turn on (as lights)...........ehn-sehn-DEHR
                (encender)
        (as water).................ah-BREER
                (abrir)
undress....................dehs-behs-TEER
                (desvestir)
use.............................oo-SAHR
                (usar)
visit........................bee-see-TAHR
                (visitar)
wait (for)...................ehs-pay-RAHR
                (esperar)
wake up....................dehs-pehr-TAHR
                (despertar)
walk.............................ahn-DAHR
                (andar)
    or.........................kah-mee-NAHR
                (caminar)
want.............................kay-REHR
                (querer)
    or.........................day-say-AHR
                (desear)
wash.............................lah-BAHR
                (lavar)
```

58

```
wear...............................yay-BAHR
                (llevar)
work.........................trah-bah-HAHR
                (trabajar)
worth (to be)......................bah-LEHR
                (valer)
write........................ehs-kree-BEER
                (escribir)
```

COMMANDS

The following commands are most useful.
Like numbers, you may wish to memorize
them. Some of them will be repeated at the
beginning of the chapter in which they will
be used the most...just as a refresher in
case you do not learn them now.

```
Bring me____ ...............TRY-gah-may____.
            (Traígame____.)
Call____ ......................YAH-may____.
            (Llame____.)
Clean____ .................LEEM-pee⌢ay____.
            (Limpie____.)
Close____ .................See⌢AY-rray____.
            (Cierre____.)
Come here................BEHN-gah ah-KEY.
            (Venga aquí.)
Come in.........................EHN-tray.
            (Entre.)
Do not worry.......Noh say pray-oh-KOO-pay.
            (No se preocupe.)
Drive around____.
    .........Day OO-nah BWEHL-tah pohr____.
        (Dé una vuelta por____.)
Drive through____ .........PAH-say pohr____.
            (Pase por____.)
Empty____ ..................BAH-see⌢ay____.
            (Vacie____.)
Get out.......................SAHL-gah.
            (Salga.)
```

```
Give me_____ ................DAY-may_____.
        (Déme_____.)
Go away....................BAH-yah-say.
        (Váyase.)
Go with_____ ..............BAH-yah kohn_____.
        (Vaya con_____.)
Help!.......................¡Ah-YOO-dah!
        (¡Ayuda!)
   or.......................¡Soh-KOH-rroh!
        (¡Socorro!)
Help yourself........SEER-bah-say oos-TEHD.
        (Sírvase ud.)
Hurry up!.................¡Ah-POO-ray-say!
        (¡Apúrese!)
Let us go...................BAH-mohs.
        (Vamos.)
Listen.....................Ehs-KOO-chay.
        (Escuche.)
Look.......................MEE-ray.
        (Mire.)
Look out!...................¡Kwee-DAH-doh!
        (¡Cuidado!)
Mail_____ ..................MAHN-day_____.
        (Mande_____.)
Open_____ ..................AH-brah_____.
        (Abra_____.)
Pass me_____ ..............PAH-say-may_____.
        (Páseme_____.)
Polish_____ ...........SAH-kay BREE-yoh_____.
        (Saque brillo_____.)
Put_____here....POHN-gah oos-TEHD_____ah-KEE.
        (Ponga ud._____aquí.)
Repeat.....................Ray-PEE-tay.
        (Repite.)
   or, Say again...........MAHN-day.
        (Mande.)
Rinse_____ ................Ehn-WHAH-gay_____.
        (Enjuague_____.)
Scrub_____ ................Ehs-TRAY-gay_____.
        (Estregue_____.)
Send (a person)............MAHN-day_____.
        (Mande_____.)
```

Send it to____.

...............SEER-bah-say-loh ah____.

      (Sírvaselo a____.)

or................MAHN-day-loh ah____.

      (Mándelo a____.)

Show me____ ....MWAYS-tray-may____.

      (Muéstreme____.)

Speak more slowly.

..........AH-blay mahs dehs-PAH-see-oh.

      (Hable más despacio.)

Stop!............................¡PAH-ray!

      (¡Pare!)

Take me to____..........YAY-bay-may ah____.

      (Lléveme a____.)

Tell me____...............DEE-gah-may____.

      (Dígame____.)

Wait for me...............Ehs-PAY-ray-may.

      (Espéreme.)

Wash____.....................LAH-bay____.

      (Lave____.)

Wax____...................Ehn-SAY-ray____.

      (Encere____.)

Wrap it up............Ehm-pah-KAY-tay-loh.

      (Empaquételo.)

CONTRASTS

a little bit...................poh-KEE-toh

      (poquito)

  a lot.........................MOO-choh

      (mucho)

beautiful.....................boh-NEE-tah

      (bonita)

  ugly..............................FAY-oh

      (feo)

before........................AHN-tays day

      (antes de)

  after....................dehs-PWAYS day

      (después de)

```
better...........................may-HOHR
                (mejor)
    worse........................pay⌢OHR
                (peor)
big (large)......................GRAHN-day
                (grande)
    small........................pay-KAY-nyoh
                (pequeño)
    little.......................CHEE-koh
                (chico)
cheap............................bah-RAH-toh
                (barato)
    expensive....................KAH-roh
                (caro)
clean............................LEEM-pee⌢oh
                (limpio)
    dirty........................SOO-see⌢oh
                (sucio)
delicious........................sah-BROH-sah
                (sabrosa)
    awful........................tay-RREE-blay
                (terrible)
early............................tehm-PRAH-noh
                (temprano)
    late.........................TAHR-day
                (tarde)
easy.............................FAH-seel
                (fácil)
    difficult....................dee-FEE-seel
                (difícil)
enough...........................bahs-TAHN-tay
                (bastante)
    too much.....................day-mah-see⌢AH-doh
                (demasiado)
fat..............................GOHR-doh
                (gordo)
    thin.........................dehl-GAH-doh
                (delgado)
forward..........................ah-day-LAHN-tay
                (adelante)
    backward.....................ah-TRAHS
                (atrás)
```

```
full...............................YAY-noh
              (lleno)
    empty........................bah-SEE-oh
              (vacío)
good...............................BWAY-noh
              (bueno)
    bad............................MAH-loh
              (malo)
heavy..........................pay-SAH-doh
              (pesado)
    light......................lee-HAY-roh
              (ligero)
here...............................ah-KEE
              (aquí)
    or.............................ah-KAH
              (acá)
    there.........................ah-YEE
              (allí)
    or.............................ah-YAH
              (allá)
high..............................AHL-toh
              (alto)
    low...........................BAH-hoh
              (bajo)
hot........................kah-lee-EHN-tay
              (caliente)
    cold...........................FREE-oh
              (frío)
long.............................LAHR-goh
              (largo)
    short.........................KOHR-toh
              (corto)
more (than)......................mahs (kay)
              (más que)
    less (than)..............MAY-nohs (kay)
              (menos que)
much.............................MOO-choh
              (mucho)
    many.........................MOO-chohs
              (muchos)
    some..........................OO-nohs
              (unos)
```

```
near (to)....................SEHR-kah (day)
              (cerca de)
    far (from)...............LAY-hohs (day)
              (lejos de)
next........................PROH-ksee-moh
              (próximo)
    last.....................OOL-tee-moh
              (último)
now.........................ah-OH-rah
              (ahora)
    then....................ehn-TOHN-sehs
              (entonces)
old..........................bee‑AY-hoh
              (viejo)
    young....................HOH-behn
              (joven)
old.........................ahn-TEE-gwoh
              (antiguo)
    new.....................NWAY-boh
              (nuevo)
open.......................ah-bee‑EHR-toh
              (abierto)
    closed.................say-RRAH-doh
              (cerrado)
push.......................ehm-POO-hay
              (empuje)
    pull...................HAH-lay
              (jale)
quick (fast)...............RAH-pee-doh
              (rápido)
    slow..................dehs-PAH-see‑oh
              (despacio)
right......................koh-REHK-toh
              (correcto)
    wrong................ay-kee-boh-KAH-doh
              (equivocado)
right......................day-RAY-chah
              (derecha)
    left..................ees-kee‑EHR-dah
              (izquierda)
    straight ahead.........day-RAY-choh
              (derecho)
```

```
vacant...........................LEE-bray
              (libre)
    occupied................oh-koo-PAH-doh
              (ocupado)
wide.............................AHN-chah
              (ancha)
    narrow.................ahn-GOHS-toh
              (angosto)
with..................................kohn
              (con)
    without..........................seen
              (sin)
yes...................................see
              (sí)
    no.................................noh
              (no)
up.........................ah-RREE-bah
              (arriba)
    down......................ah-BAH-hoh
              (abajo)
outside.....................ah-FWAY-rah
              (afuera)
    inside...................ah-DEHN-troh
              (adentro)
```

The last four words--arriba, abajo, afuera,
adentro--are a popular toast. And, I imagine you could use one about now!

FAMILY

When you go on a vacation, you probably will have companions: your spouse, brother, sister, children, friends or even your pet. These are the words you need to introduce them.

This is my____...EHS-toh (-ah) ehs mee____.
    (Esto (-a) es mi____.)

family........................fah-MEE-lee-ah
            (familia)
Mr............................say-NYOHR
            (señor)
Mrs...........................say-NYOH-rah
            (señora)
Miss..........................say-nyoh-REE-tah
            (señorita
a boy in his teens............moo-CHAH-choh
            (muchacho)
a girl until she's a señorita
........................moo-CHAH-chah
            (muchacha)
a boy from infancy until he's a muchacho
..............................NEE-nyoh
            (niño)
a girl from infancy until she's a muchacha
..............................NEE-nyah
            (niña)
babies........................NAY-nays
            (nenes)
    or........................bay-BAYS
            (bebés)
mother........................MAH-dray
            (madre, f)
mama..........................mah-MAH
            (mamá)
father........................PAH-dray
            (padre, m)
papa..........................pah-PAH
            (papá)

```
parents..........................PAH-drays
              (padres, m)
husband.......................mah-REE-doh
              (marido)
   or.........................ehs-POH-soh
              (esposo)
wife..........................ehs-POH-sah
              (esposa)
brother (sister)..............ehr-MAH-noh
              (hermano, -a)
children (all male)................EE-hohs
              (hijos)
         (all female)..............EE-hahs
              (hijas)
         (one or more of each)......EE-hohs
              (hijos)
```

(In any case where masculine and feminine nouns are used together, the plural ending is always masculine plural.)

```
aunt..............................TEE^ah
              (tía)
uncle.............................TEE^oh
              (tío)
cousin...........................PREE-moh
              (primo, -a)
nephew (niece)................soh-BREE-noh
              (sobrino, -a)
grandchild.....................nee^AY-toh
              (nieto, -a)
brother- or sister-in-law......koo-NYAH-doh
              (cuñado, -a)
friend.........................ah-MEE-goh
              (amigo, -a)
sweetheart or fiancé.............NOH-bee^oh
              (novio)
   fianceé......................NOH-bee^ah
              (novia)
relative...................pah-ree^EHN-tay
              (pariente)
```

```
bird.........................PAH-hah-roh
             (pájaro)
cat..............................GAH-toh
             (gato)
dog...........................PAY-rroh
             (perro)
```

If you're traveling with kids, you might find these commands helpful. I know I have.

```
Be quiet...............KAH-yay lah BOH-kah.
          (Calle la boca.)
Silence...................See-LEHN-see-oh.
          (Silencio.)
Sit down..................See-EHN-teh-say.
          (Siéntese.)
```

QUANTITIES AND CONVERSIONS

In Mexico, Europe, and soon to be in the U.S.--the metric system. The following words and lists are for those of you who, like me, have avoided learning them in the hopes that maybe, just maybe, the change-over will not happen, at least not in our lifetime. Then when we do go abroad, not only is there a new language to cope with, there are unfamiliar terms for distances, weights and measures. One of these days, I am going to learn them. Perhaps--mañana.

```
inch..........................pool-GAH-doh
             (pulgado)
     = 2.54 centimeters
foot..............................pee-AY
             (pie)
     = .3048 meter
mile.............................MEE-yah
             (milla)
     = 1.6093 kilometers
yard........................= .9144 meter
```

```
gallon.............................gah-LOHN
                (galón)
quart................= .9463 liter (liquid)
pound..............................LEE-brah
                (libra)
    = .4536 kilogram
ton (in Mexico, also refers to metric ton)
    ......................toh-nay-LAH-dah
                (tonelada)
meter.............................MAY-troh
                (metro)
kilometer.................kee-LOH-may-troh
                (kilómetro)
liter.............................LEE-troh
                (litro)
milliliter................mee-lee-LEE-troh
                (mililitro)
gram..............................GRAH-moh
                (gramo)
kilo..............................KEE-loh
                (kilo)
```

KILOGRAMS TO POUNDS

Pounds	Kilograms
2.2	1
4.41	2
6.61	3
8.82	4
11.02	5
13.23	6
15.43	7
17.64	8
19.84	9
22.05	10
33.23	15
44.09	20
55.12	25
66.14	30
88.18	40
110.23	50

LITERS TO GALLONS

Gallons	Liters
1	3.78
2	7.57
3	11.36
4	15.14
5	18.93
6	22.71
7	26.50
8	30.28
9	34.06
10	37.85
15	56.78
20	75.71
25	94.64
30	113.55
40	151.40
50	189.25

The monetary rate of exchange fluctuates--
especially recently with the Mexican peso.
Drastic changes can occur in a short period
of time and the result is utter chaos...
which I witnessed in Puerto Vallarta during
one of the peso devaluations. Bargains are
abundant when this happens but if you've
already exchanged the majority of your
American dollars into pesos, you, too, end
up losing.

How much you need to exchange before you leave the States or on a daily or weekly basis once you're there, depends on personal buying or spending habits and where you are going. To know precisely how much money to exchange is a guessing game but you should exchange some amount because although border towns and cities generally will accept U.S. dollars, in most villages, pesos are the only currency acknowledged.

Try to exchange only what you think you will use. You lose money each time you make a money exchange. To make this loss less when purchasing items, try to get U.S. dollars in change when you pay in U.S. dollars and pesos in change when buying with pesos.

Travelers' checks, although readily cashed when touring the U.S., are not accepted in Mexico at gasoline stations, small cafes and most stores or restaurants. Banks and large hotels can cash them for you. Travelers' checks of smaller denominations are best because many businesses do not keep large amounts of cash on hand.

The Mexican monetary system is based on the peso which is divided into 100 units called centavos. Current Mexican coin denominations are 10-, 20- and 50-centavos, and one-, five- and 10-pesos. You have to look closely at the coins before you hand them out because several are similar in size but vary considerably in worth.

Banknotes begin at 20 pesos but there are still some 10 peso bills in use that are slowly being replaced by coins of the same denomination. Mexico uses the same symbol ($) to denote its currency as the U.S. uses for dollars. The first time you see a price tag or study a menu, you will undoubtedly gasp: the amounts seem tremendous. Just remember to convert it into pesos and things return to a proper perspective.

There are two ways to make conversions easier. One is to make a table of equivalents on a piece of paper and take it with you. The other is to carry a credit card-size calculator. Either way will give you quick conversions.

Currently, because the value of the peso is in such a state of flux, pesos are difficult to exchange at U.S. banks. However, the international currency exchanges located on the U.S. side, near to the border, have the best rate I have found. This rate varies from store to store so shop for the best one available that day. If you are exchanging large amounts of money, negotiate for the best rate. Currency exchanges are also found at major airports servicing Mexico although the rate of exchange is not as favorable.

In Mexico, U.S. currency can be converted into pesos at most banks, money exchanges, large hotels, some grocery stores or restaurants.

Money exhanges at banks are made only during certain hours of the day, generally first thing in the morning. Bank hours in Mexico are different than those you're accustomed to. Most banks open at 8 or 9 a.m., close for the day sometime between noon and 2 p.m. and are not open on any Mexican holidays (of which there are many and few coincide with our recognized days off). Also, the Banco National de Mexico

(Banamex) will send and accept wired funds. Arrangements should be made through the bank and the local telegraph office.

A 'casa de cambio' is a store whose sole business is money exchange. They are open most of the day, except for the variable lunch hour, and frequently at night.

VOCABULARY

Can you exchange____dollars?
.¿PWAY-day kahm-bee⌢AHR____DOH-lah-rays?
(¿Puede cambiar____dólares?)
Exchange it, please.
........KAHM-bee⌢ay-loh, pohr fah-BOHR.
(Cámbielo, por favor.)
Where can I change American dollars?
........¿DOHN-day PWAY-doh kahm-bee⌢AHR
DOH-lah-rays ah-may-ree-KAH-nohs?
(¿Dónde puedo cambiar dólares
americanos?)
I want to change____dollars.
............Kee-see⌢AIR-ah kahm-bee⌢AHR
____DOH-lah-rays.
(Quisera cambiar____dólares.)
What is the rate of exchange?
........¿Kwahl ehs ehl KAHM-bee⌢oh pohr
DOH-lah-rays?
(¿Cuál es el cambio por dólares?)
Will you accept travelers checks?
¿Ah-SEHP-tah CHAY-kays bee⌢ah-HAY-rohs?
(¿Acepta cheques viajeros?)
Sign here.................FEER-may ah-KEE.
(Firme aquí.)
to accept....................ah-seph-TAHR
(aceptar)
bank..........................BAHN-koh
(banco)
cashiers check.........CHAY-kay day KAH-hah
(cheque (m) de caja)

74

```
cent.........................sehn-TAH-boh
              (centavo)
   to change.................kahm-bee-AHR
              (cambiar)
current rate of exchange
   ............KAHM-bee-oh koh-rree-EHN-tay
           (cambio corriente)
dollar...........................DOH-lahr
              (dólar)
house of exchange...KAH-sah day KAHM-bee-oh
           (casa de cambio)
money order........................HEE-roh
              (giro)
personal check..CHAY-kays pehr-soh-NAH-lays
           (cheques personales)
peso..............................PEH-soh
rate of today.........KAHM-bee-oh day OH-ee
           (cambio de hoy)
travelers checks.............CHAY-kays day
              bee-ah-HAY-roh
           (cheques de viajero)
```

MAIL

The Post Office and the Telegraph Office
are either in the same building or close to
each other. Postcards, postage-paid enve-
lopes and stamps are sold and letters and
packages are mailed in the Post Office.
Messages and money can be sent and received
in the Telegraph Office.

Letters or packages can be sent air mail,
special (which means special handling, not
special delivery), registered (there is no
certified mail service in Mexico) or in-
sured.

You may mail gifts not exceeding $25 in
retail value to persons in the U.S. without
paying duty or taxes. As many gifts as

desired may be sent provided the total value of the packages mailed to one person in one day does not exceed $25. The words gift enclosed and the value of the contents, in large letters, should be written on the outside of the package. You may not mail alcoholic beverages, tobacco products or any perfume valued at more than $1.

You can receive letters through General Delivery in any city, town or village. Be sure to have all mail sent to you via air mail, otherwise you may not get it before you leave a particular area. A list of those who have received mail is posted each day and is usually displayed for a week. After that length of time, the letter is returned to the sender.

The person sending you the letter should address the envelope as follows:

Your Name
La Lista Correo
City, State
Mexico

If you are staying in a big city that has good transportation to a nearby smaller town, have your mail sent there. The list has fewer names to sort through and you can get in and out quicker.

Identification may be required before picking up the mail so be sure to take some with you.

TELEGRAMS

To mail a telegram, first write the message on the form in the office, give it to the clerk and ask him, "How much?" Pay the proper amount and make sure the clerk can read the message. The fastest way to send it is <u>Ordinario.</u>

If you receive money by telegram, pick up the telegram at one window, take it to the window labeled <u>giros</u>, money orders, and exchange it for the money. For this transaction, <u>you</u> <u>will</u> <u>need</u> <u>positive</u> <u>identification.</u>

In case of an emergency, messages can be sent by the government radio which has terminals in most communities.

VOCABULARY

Where is____?........¿DOHN-day ehs-TAH____?
       (¿Dónde está____?)
I need____ ....Nay-say-SEE-toh____.
       (Necesito____.)
Send this____ ....MAHN-day EHS-tay____.
       (Mande este____.)
How much?....................¿KWAHN-toh?
       (¿Cuánto?)
Is there duty?..........¿Eye ehm-PWAYS-toh?
       (¿Hay empuesto?)
address...................dee-rehk-see^OHN
       (dirección)
air mail..........koh-RRAY-oh ah^EH-ray^oh
       (correo aéreo)
air mail stamps
    ....TEEM-brays day ah^EH-ray^oh
       (timbres de aéreo)
by air mail...............pohr ah-bee^OHN
       (por avión)
cable office...oh-fee-SEE-nah day KAH-blays
       (oficina de cables)
  to cable..........kah-blay-grah-fee^AHR
       (cablegrafiar)
city.......................see^oo-DAHD
       (ciudad, f)

```
envelopes.........................SOH-brays
                (sobres, m)
general delivery list
    ...................LEES-tah koh-RRAY⁻oh
            (lista correo)
insured.................ah-say-goo-RAH-doh
            (asegurado)
letter............................KAHR-tah
                (carta)
mail box..................ah-pahr-TAH-doh
            (apartado)
    or...........................boo-SOHN
            (buzón, m)
message.......................mehn-SAH-hay
                (mensaje, m)
money order.......................HEE-roh
                (giro)
North American..nohr-tay-ah-may-ree-KAHN-oh
            (norteamericano)
ordinario................ohr-dee-NAH-ree⁻oh
package.........................pah-KAY-tay
                (paquete, m)
post card...........tahr-HAY-tah pohs-TAHL
            (tarjeta postal)
post office...................koh-RRAY⁻oh
                (correo)
registered...............ray-hees-TRAH-doh
            (registrado)
special....................ehs-pay-see⁻AHL
            (especial)
stamps..........................TEEM-brays
                (timbres, f)
    or...........................SAY-yohs
                (sellos)
state.........................ehs-TAH-doh
                (estado)
telegram..................tay-lay-GRAH-mah
            (telegrama, m)
    to telegraph........tay-lay-grah-fee⁻AHR
                (telegrafiar)
telegraph office..........tay-LAY-grah-fohs
                (el telégrafos)
```

United States
..........lohs ehs-TAH-dohs oo-NEE-dohs
(los estados unidos)

TELEPHONE

I wish I could have figured out a device
similar to what the Spaniards have in their
pay phone booths for my loquacious teen-
agers. I would have made money and been
able to use my own phone when I wanted it--
instead of waiting for a far-too-long con-
versation to end.

The person calling first must purchase
fichas, chips, to make a phone call. The
coin is deposited and while you speak you
watch it slowly descending a see-through
tube. When the token reaches the bottom of
the slide, the call is ended...whether you
are or not.

Making phone calls in Mexico is not difficult, only time-consuming. In Cabo San
Lucas, for example, long distance phone
calls can be placed only during designated
morning hours at the telephone exchange.
You wait your turn along with the dozen or
more Americans who also want to call home.

You can pay for the call when you make it,
but incredible as it seems, it is cheaper
to call collect. Be sure to make arrangements with someone in the States to accept
your calls.

For the sake of clarity, say each number
individually: 1-2-3-4 is uno, dos, tres,
cuatro.

VOCABULARY

I want to call___ ...Kee⌢AIR-oh yah-MAHR___ .
        (Quiero llamar___ .)
   collect................PAH-rah koh-BRAHR
         (para cobrar)
   long distance..LAHR-gah dees-TAHN-see⌢ah
         (larga distancia)
   the U.S....lohs ehs-TAH-dohs oo-NEE-dohs
         (los estados unidos)
   (E.E.U.U...abbreviation for the U.S.)

If you receive a phone call, respond with:
   hello..........................BWAY-noh
                (bueno)
      or.........................DEE-gah
                  (diga)
      or.................¿Kee⌢EHN AH-blah?
         (¿Quién habla?)

Thank you for your trouble.
     .....MOO-chas GRAH-see⌢ahs pohr soo
         ah-tehn-see⌢OHN.
   (Muchas gracias por su atención.)
You have a wrong number.
     ....Tee⌢AY-nay ehl NOO-may-roh
        eh-kee-boh-KAH-doh.
    (Tiene el número equivocado.)

to telephone............tay-lay-foh-nay-AHR

At last, free time to explore, see what's
just around the corner, try out your Spanish, eat a meal out, buy gifts, or reprovi-
sion. And are you in for a treat! Each town
has its own flavor, distinct characteris-
tics, and, in some areas, unique dress.
It's an adventure that's bound to provide
entertaining stories for the folks back
home.

In Turtle Bay, Baja, a small community whose livelihood centers around the government-owned fish cannery, are small stores scattered about the six block radius of the center...and a tiny native restaurant that serves a complete lobster dinner for $5. In Guaymas, a block square enclosed 'mercado' holds everything from baby chicks in small cardboard carry-home containers to vegetables, meats, poultry and clothing. Near the shopping center in Acapulco, dark-skinned Indians wrapped in colorful blankets, display vibrantly painted wall hangings created on a heavy, paper-like material made from tree bark.

Indeed, a trip to town is adventure of the highest commendation. Unfortunately, I know those Americans who find such outings distasteful. "It isn't like the U.S.," they mutter. Of course, it isn't--it's Mexico, it's Spain, it's a foreign country.

Yes, it's different: it can be hot, dusty, public rest room facilities inadequate, and you need to be careful about what you eat or drink. You'll hear a cacophony of unfamiliar sounds, smell a variety of unusual odors, get lost, become bewildered and return totally exhausted. But, the more you go out, the more you communicate, the more enjoyable and easier it is.

TAXIS

Riding in a taxi lets you sit back (notice I didn't say relax) and enjoy the scenery. The driver is familiar with the terrain and is most helpful with local knowledge and information. But the first thing you must do, before you set a foot inside the cab, is negotiate a price.

Tell him where you want to go--naturally, you won't know the exact location--but tell him the type of store and ask him, "How much?" At first, you may think you could be taken for the proverbial 'ride' but I have found few drivers who are dishonest. Most try to get you wherever by the shortest way possible.

If the price sounds reasonable, and cabs are far less expensive in Mexico than the States, agree, and you're on your way. If you think it's too high, try negotiating. He can't say anything more than "No."

Cab drivers also can be hired for the whole day or to wait for you while you do extensive shopping. The latter happens to me frequently. Delivering boats to and from Mexico requires provisioning somewhere along the way. Sometimes I must totally provision which means many, MANY sacks of groceries and numerous stops at small stores to get the necessary items. In Puerto Vallarta, I hired a cab driver to wait while I shopped, stop at four or five different businesses and take three of us to the yacht harbor--a good 10 miles from town. The total cost was about $8.

In Spain, look for the cabs that are black with a red stripe. These are government regulated vehicles so the price is consistent. Around town, and in particular, near the airport, you will see solid black cabs. These are not government regulated so the fares can be whatever the driver wants to charge.

In Mexico City, the Pesero cabs (called peseros because they used to cost one peso) run the popular route from La Reforma to the major shopping square or zócalo and back. I understand from a recent visitor to "Mexico" (as the city is called by natives) the cost is about 20 pesos.

BUSES

Local bus service in Mexico makes the town percolate. Everyone takes them because the price is always right. That same distance from the marina in Puerto Vallarta to town was 35 U.S. cents.

Be prepared for a small amount of temporary discomfort. Buses stop everywhere; windows are open wide; you will probably have to stand, hanging from a bar or grasping a seatback; and you will sympathize with a sardine when you get off. Don't take the bus if you're dressed to the hilt and planning to look unruffled when you arrive-- take a cab.

The big question when taking a bus in an unfamiliar town is where do you get off? That's a tough one to answer. You can ask someone before you get on the bus, ask the bus driver to stop near the place or question a fellow commuter. In any event, try to squiggle your way to either door because the bus only stops for a few seconds and you want to be ready to get off as quickly as possible. If you do get off in the wrong place, it's not all that devastating. You're probably within walking distance of where you wanted to go, or, if not, there's always the ubiquitous taxi to hail.

Another bus system exists in Mexico that is used for intercity or interstate travel. These First Class buses require reservations and you may have to wait a while to catch one. If you are going any distance, be sure to wait. <u>Tres Estrellas de Oro</u>, shortened to Three Stars, is one such bus line. No one is allowed to stand, the bus is air-conditioned (if it's working) and toilet facilities are aboard (sometimes operative). Stops are made for meals or whatever. The depots are not what you had hoped but you can get off and stretch your legs.

First Class bus fares are not expensive either. I rode from El Rosario, Baja, to Tijuana, a distance of approximately 250 miles, for about $6.

I find it wise to look at the scenery, not the oncoming traffic. Although there is the familiar solid and broken yellow line down the middle of most major highways, it evidently indicates a line over which the center of a vehicle should hover. This middle-of-the-road attitude is tolerable when the highway is flat and straight but, believe me, when whizzing around blind corners through a mountainous terrain, my heart pounds furiously.

TRAINS

A train ride in Mexico can be an exciting adventure--if you're an optimist--or the most wearisome form of travel available. Look at the ticket you purchased to make sure it will take you where you want and in the class you wanted. Trains stop frequently and a 250 mile ride has been known to take up to eleven hours. Once again, go First Class if possible.

Another form of transportation in Mexico City is the <u>Metro</u>, an underground train that rides on inflated, rubber tires. It runs from the heart of downtown to nearby areas. Riding on the Metro is comfortable as well as entertaining because the station walls at each stop are covered with colorful Mexican tile mosaics.

COMMERCIAL AIRLINES

If you're planning a major off-shoot journey, flying will get you there quickly and comfortably. You need reservations. Before you make them, you might want to inquire what kind of plane you will be taking. DC-3's, DC-6's, DC-9's and Boeing 707's are active--everything from real relics to intercontinental jets.

Be sure to note the day of departure. Planes do not fly to each city every day, frequently, it's once or twice a week. Take your tourist card and passport for identification. In addition to the price of the ticket, you must pay a departure tax which helps improve runways, terminals and so forth, I'm told by officials.

Get to the airport in plenty of time because you don't check in at just one counter, you must check in at several. Airports can vary slightly in procedure but, the following is the most common sequence of events. First, go to the ticket counter where you show the ticket and leave your luggage, then to the clerk who handles the departure tax and writes down the amount due. Proceed to the clerk who receives the money and gives you stamps for your money. Then return to the ticket agent to finalize the transaction.

If you are initiating a trip from a Mexican border town, the procedure is different. First you check in with the ticket agent who takes your luggage and tags it. Follow the other steps listed above. After returning to the ticket agent, take your tourist card to Immigration where it will be stamped and one page removed. Go to Customs where your baggage is now setting. At this time, it may or may not be inspected. If you have other than personal items, you might have to pay some amount of money to the agent to process you through. (For information on 'mordida,' see page 222.) You are now ready for departure.

OTHER FORMS OF TRANSPORTATION

In Mazatlán, surreys with the fringe on top run about the superb beachfront area from one end to the other. Prices are reasonable and sometimes negotiable. If it's a sun-shiny day, the ride is most enjoyable.

Major cities have rent-a-car establishments. If you decide to lease a car, read the chapter CARS AND RV's for details about driving in Mexico. Sight-seeing bus tours are available in large cities. Check with a hotel or Department of Tourism for details and schedules.

Off-road "Safari's," Volkswagen's version of the Jeep, are for rent. If you like exploring the back country, look into leasing one.

Running from mainland Mexico to Baja--or vice versa--is the passenger and auto ferry service. If you plan to ship your car, you need a car permit that is available at all ferry ports. The same documents required to get your car into Mexico are necessary to obtain this permit. Ferry reservations should be made in advance; however, be aware that although you took the trouble to schedule your trip in advance, reservations may not be honored. Pets are permitted on ferries by showing the approved Health Certificate you already have.

VOCABULARY

How often does the bus go by?
...........¿Kay tahn say-GEE-doh PAH-sah
            ehl ow-toh-BOOS?
    (¿Qué tan seguido pasa el autobús?)
How much is the fare?
    ....¿KWAHN-toh KWEHS-tah ehl pah-SAH-hay?
        (¿Cuánto cuesta el pasaje?)
I want to go to____..Kee-AIR-oh eer ah____.
            (Quiero ir a____.)
Where do I get off?
    ....¿DOHN-day DAY-boh bah-HAHR?
            (¿Dónde debo bajar?)
Tell me where to get off.
    ...DEE-gah-may DOHN-day DAY-boh bah-HAHR.
        (Dígame donde debo bajar.)
Get off here...............BAH-hay ah-KEE.
                (Baje aquí.)
Take me to____..........YAY-bay-may ah____.
            (Lléveme a____.)
Drive around the city.
    Day OO-nah BWEHL-tah pohr la see-oo-DAHD.
        (Dé una vuelta por la ciudad.)
Drive through the shopping district.
    ....PAH-sah pohr ehl SEHN-troh.
            (Pasa por el centro.)
Go to the____..........BAH-yah ah lah____.
            (Vaya a la____.)
    right...................day-RAY-chah.
                (derecha)

```
left................ees-kee-EHR-dah.
          (izquierda)
Go straight ahead.....SEE-gah day-RAY-choh.
          (Siga derecho.)
Stop here.................PAH-ray ah-KEE.
          (Pare aquí.)
Wait for me...............Ehs-PAY-ray-may.
          (Espéreme.)
```

What time does the___leave for___?
..........¿Ah kay OH-rah SAH-lay ehl____
          PAH-rah____?
(¿A qué hora sale el___para___?)

What time does ___ arrive?
..........¿Ah kay OH-rah YAY-gah ah___?
          (¿A qué hora llega a___?)

Does the___stop in___?
.................¿PAH-rah___ehn___?
          (¿Para___en___?)

I need___tickets to___.
    Nay-say-SEE-toh___bee-YAY-tays ah___.
       (Necesito___billetes a___.)

Is there room?.........¿Eye ehs-PAH-see-oh?
          (¿Hay espacio?)

When does___it leave?
................¿KWAHN-doh SAH-lay____?
          (¿Cuándo sale___?)

When does it arrive?
..................¿KWAHN-doh YAY-gah?
          (¿Cuándo llega?)

What kind of plane?
..........¿Kay KLAH-say day ah-bee-OHN?
          (¿Que clase de avión?)

Which train?.................¿Kwahl trehn?
          (¿Cuál tren?)

I want my baggage checked.
Kee-AIR-oh fahk-too-RAHR mees mah-LAY-tahs.
    (Quiero facturar mis maletas.)

Open the window...AH-brah lah behn-TAH-nah.
          (Abra la ventana.)

Close the window.
..........See-AY-rray lah behn-TAH-nah.
          (Cierre la ventana.)

                    89

```
All Aboard!.....................¡LEES-tohs!
                (¡Listos!)
   or.........................¡Ah BOHR-doh!
                (¡A bordo!)
airplane........................ah-bee‿OHN
                (avión, m)
airport.................ah‿ay-roh-PWERH-toh
                (aeropuerto)
avenue......................ah-bay-NEE-dah
                (avenida)
baggage.....................mah-LAY-tahs
                (maletas)
   or.......................ay-kee-PAH-hay
                (equipaje, m)
   checks..............kohm-proh-BAHN-tays
                (comprobantes, m)
bicycle..................bee-see-KLAY-tah
                (bicicleta)
block..........................KWAH-droh
                (cuadro)
bus...........................ow-toh-BOOHS
                (autobús, m)
   in Puerto Rico.................GWAH-gwah
                (guagua)
   station
        ehs-tah-see‿OHN day ow-toh-BOOS-ays
        (estación (f) de autobuses)
cab, taxi........................TAHK-see
                (taxi, m)
corner........................ehs-KEE-nah
                (esquina)
downtown....................ahl SEHN-troh
                (al centro)
first class..........pree-MAY-roh KLAH-say
                (primero clase)
   second class.......say-GOON-doh KLAH-say
                (segundo clase)
Metro..........................MAY-troh
motorcycle............moh-toh-see-KLAY-tah
                (motocicleta)
   or...........................MOH-toh
                (moto)
```

```
occupied....................oh-koo-PAH-doh
              (ocupado)
on time....................ah tee-EHM-poh
              (a tiempo)
pesero.......................peh-SAY-roh
station...................ehs-tah-see-OHN
              (estación, f)
stop (for bus, train)...........pah-RAH-dah
              (parada)
street...........................KAH-yay
              (calle, f)
ticket.......................bee-YAY-tay
              (billete, m)
   one way.........................EE-dah
                (ida)
   round trip...........EE-dah ee BWEHL-tah
              (ida y vuelta)
   office...oh-fee-SEE-nah day bee-YAY-tays
         (oficina de billetes)
time table...................oh-RAH-ree-oh
              (horario)
tip (money)..................proh-PEE-nah
              (propina)
train................................trehn
              (tren, m)
   or...................fay-rroh-kah-REEL
            (ferrocaril, m)
Three Stars............Trehs Ehs-TRAY-yahs
           (Tres Estrellas)
vacant..........................LEE-bray
              (libre)
```

DOWNTOWN

Downtown--Petula Clark made it famous in a
record several years ago and for a good
reason--that is where the action is! From
museums, historical sites, religious monu-
ments, and specialized stores for day-time
activities to caberets, the opera or thea-
ter after dark. For sport enthusiasts,

there is jai alai in the Frontón Palace or
the bull fights in the outdoor rings.

There is definitely something for everyone!

VOCABULARY

How much is the admission?
    ¿KWAHN-toh KWEHS-tah lah ehn-TRAH-dah?
      (¿Cuánto cuesta la entrada?)
Is the admission free?
    ¿Ehs lah ehn-TRAH-dah grah-too‑EE-tah?
      (¿Es la entrada gratuita?)
Is it open on (Sunday)?
    ....¿Ehs-TAH ah-bee‑EHR-toh lohs
            (doh-MEEN-gohs)?
      (¿Está abierto los (domingos)?
    Closed Sundays
      ......Say-RRAH-doh lohs doh-MEEN-gohs
          (Cerrado los domingos)

Where are the seats?
    ¿DOHN-day ehs-TAHN lohs ah-see‑EHN-tohs?
      (¿Dónde están los asientos?)
    In the center?.......¿Ehn ehl SEHN-troh?
          (¿En el centro?)
    In the rear?.............¿Ahl FOHN-doh?
          (¿Al fondo?)
    In a box?.............¿Ehn ehl PAHL-koh?
          (¿En el palco?)
    In the balcony?.¿Ehn lah gah-lay-REE‑ah?
          (¿En la galería?)

What time does the show start?
    ....¿Ah kay OH-rah koh-mee‑EHN-sah
        ehl ehs-pehk-TAH-koo-loh?
    (¿A qué hora comienza el espectáculo?)
What time is it over?
    ....¿Ah kay OH-rah ah-KAH-bah
        ehl ehs-pehk-TAH-koo-loh?
      (¿A qué hora acaba el espectáculo?)

```
admission.....................ehn-TRAH-dah
              (entrada)
auto parts.......ray-fahk-see‐ohn-ahr-EE‐ah
             (refaccionaría)
bakery...................pah-nah-dehr-EE‐ah
               (panadería)
bank............................BAHN-koh
               (banco)
barbershop..............pay-loo-kehr-EE‐ah
              (peluquería)
beauty parlor......sah-LOHN day bay-YAY-sah
          (salon de belleza)
book store................lee-brehr-EE‐ah
               (librería)
bullfight.........koh-RREE-dah day TOH-rohs
           (corrida de toros)
candy store...............dool-sehr-EE‐ah
               (dulcería)
car wash, body shop.....kah-rroh-sehr-EE‐ah
             (carrocería)
cathedral...................kah-tay-DRAHL
               (catedral, m)
chamber of commerce
     .........KAH-mah-rah day koh-MEHR-see‐oh
          (cámara de comercio)
church......................ee-GLAY-see‐ah
               (iglesia)
    catholic...............kah-TOH-lee-kah
               (católica)
        mass.........................MEE-sah
               (misa)
    protestant............proh-tehs-TAHN-tay
           (protestante, m)
        service..............sehr-BEE-see‐oh
               (servicio)
city.........................see‐oo-DAHD
               (ciudad, f)
    small city.................poh-BLAH-dah
               (poblada)
city hall....pah-LAH-see‐oh goh-bee‐EHR-noh
            (palacio gobierno)
```

93

```
clinic........................KLEE-nee-kah
              (clínica)
clothing store..............roh-pehr-EE^ah
              (ropería)
conasupo....................koh-nah-SOO-poh
    (government charter grocery store)

cover charge...............koo-bee^EHR-toh
              (cubierto)
customs.......................ah-DWAH-nah
              (aduana)
Department of Tourism
   ..day-pahr-tah-MEHN-toh day too-REES-moh
          (departamento de turismo)
department store...................bah-SAHR
              (bazar, m)
downtown......................ahl SEHN-troh
              (al centro)
drugstore......................boh-TEE-kah
              (botica)
   or......................fahr-MAH-see^ah
              (farmacia)
dry cleaning store.........teen-tohr-EE^ah
              (tintoría)
dry goods..................ahl-mah-SAY-nays
              (almacenes, m)
embassy.....................ehm-bah-HAH-dah
              (embajada)
entrance......................ehn-TRAH-dah
              (entrada)
exit..........................sah-LEE-dah
              (salida)
fish market.............pehs-kah-dehr-EE^ah
              (pescadería)
floor show............ehs-pehk-TAH-koo-loh
              (espectáculo)
fruit store................froo-tehr-EE^ah
              (frutería)
gasoline station........gah-soh-lee-NAY-rah
              (gasolinera)
general store..............koh-MEHR-see^oh
              (comercio)
```

grocery store..............ah-boh-RROH-tays
              (aborrotes, m)
hairdresser....................pay-nah-DOHR
              (peinador, -a)
hardware..............fay-rray-tehr-EE‿ah
              (ferretería)
hat store.............sohm-bray-rehr-EE‿ah
              (sombrerería)
hospital......................ohs-pee-TAHL
              (hospital, m)
ice cream store.........ay-lah-dehr-EE‿ah
              (heladería)
ice house..................nay-behr-EE‿ah
              (nevería)
immigration............een-mee-grah-see‿OHN
              (inmigración)
    or....................mee-grah-see‿OHN
              (migración)
jai alai.........................HI ah-lie
    (a fast-moving, action-packed sport)
    Frontón......................frohn-TOHN
              (jai alai palace)
jewelry store...............hoh-yehr-EE‿ah
              (joyería)
laundromat............lah-bahn-dehr-EE‿ah
              (lavandería)
library................bee-blee‿oh-TAY-kah
              (biblioteca)
liquor store.............lee-koh-rehr-EE‿ah
              (licorería)
lumber (wood dealer).......mah-day-RAY-roh
              (maderero)
market.......................mehr-KAH-doh
              (mercado)
    supermarket........SOO-pehr mehr-KAH-doh
              (super mercado)
meat store.............kahr-nee-sehr-EE‿ah
              (carnicería)
monument..................moh-noo-MEHN-toh
              (monumento)
motel.........................moh-TEHL
              (motel, m)

95

```
        or.......................pah-rah-DOHR
                 (parador, f)
movie......................pay-LEE-koo-lah
                 (película)
        or.............................SEE-nay
                 (cine, m)
museum........................moo-SAY-oh
                 (museo)
newsstand.....................kee-OHS-koh
                 (kiosco)
    American newspapers
    ..........pay-ree-OH-dee-kohs
        ......nohr-tay-ah-may-ree-KAH-nohs
        (periódicos norteamericanos)
    magazines...................ray-BEES-tahs
                 (revistas)
night club.....................kah-bah-REH
                 (cabaret, m)
opera..........................OH-pay-rah
                 (ópera)
orchestra.....................ohr-KEHS-tah
                 (orquesta)
park...........................PAHR-kay
                 (parque, m)
pastry shop............pahs-tay-lehr-EE-ah
                 (pastelería)
plaza..........................PLAH-sah
                 (plaza)
police.....................poh-lee-SEE-ah
                 (policía)
    police station........koh-mee-SAH-ree-oh
                 (comisario)
popsicle shop...........pah-lay-tehr-EE-ah
                 (paletería)
port captain............kah-pee-tahn-EE-ah
                 (capitanía)
post office....................koh-RREH-oh
                 (correo)
pottery store...........ahl-fah-rehr-EE-ah
                 (alfarería)
program......................proh-GRAH-mah
                 (programa, m)
```

```
repair (almost anything)...........tah-YEHR
               (taller, m)
    ....tah-YEHR day ray-pah-rah-see‿OHN-ays
          (taller de reparaciones)
restaurant..............rehs-tahoo-RAHN-tay
             (restaurante, m)
   or...........................FOHN-doh
               (fondo)
rubbish.......................bah-SOO-rah
               (basura)
saloon.......................tah-BEHR-nah
               (taberna)
   or........................kahn-TEE-nah
               (cantina)
school.......................ehs-KWAY-lah
               (escuela)
sewing goods store.........mehr-sehr-EE‿ah
             (mercería)
shoe store..............sah-pah-tehr-EE‿ah
             (zapatería)
shopping center...............mehr-KAH-doh
               (mercado)
   or..........................SOH-kah-loh
               (zócalo)
   or..........................SEHN-troh
               (centro)
stationery store........pah-pay-lehr-EE‿ah
             (papelería)
statue......................ehs-TAH-too‿ah
               (estatua)
store.........................tee‿EHN-dah
               (tienda)
theater.......................tay‿AH-troh
               (teatro)
tickets.......................bee-YAY-tays
             (billetes, m)
tile maker....................tay-HAY-roh
               (tejero)
tire store................yahn-tehr-EE‿ah
               (llantería)
```

tobacco store.............tah-bah-kehr-EE-ah
(tabaquería)
(in Spain, stamps for letters are sold
in tobacco store)
tortilla store.........tohr-tee-yehr-EE-ah
(tortillería)
vegetable store........behr-doo-lehr-EE-ah
(verdulería)
watch shop..............ray-loh-hehr-EE-ah
(relojería)
zoo..............hahr-DEEN soo-LOH-hee-koh
(jardín zoológico)

SIGNS

No smoking.........Say proh-EE-bay foo-MAHR
(Se prohibe fumar)
No admittance.....Say proh-EE-bay ehn-TRAHR
(Se prohibe entrar)
No parking
.....Say proh-EE-bay ehs-tah-see-oh-NAHR
(Se prohibe estacionar)
Keep off the grass
...............Noh pee-SAHR lah YEHR-bah
(No pisar la hierba)
Wet paint!
....¡Kwee-DAH-doh kohn lah peen-TOO-rah!
(¡Cuidado con la pintura!)

98

What size?
¿Kay tah-MAH-nyoh?
(¿Qué tamaño?)

Shopping in any foreign country, to me, is the gravy of traveling. In Mexico, each state has one or more specialty items indigenous to that area. Oaxaca, for example, uses the local clay to make the distinctive grey-black pottery for which it is so famous. The exquisitely carved wooden statues of the Seris Indians originate not too far from Guaymas. Then, there are rugs, opals, onyx, guitars, blankets, tiles and so much more.

Bargains and bargaining flourish--and it's fun looking for the former and trying your talents with the latter. If you find an item you like and think the price too high, offer the salesperson less. He'll counter offer and so it goes. I have discovered that if I move on, pick up another item and feign interest over it, the haggling over the first item takes on importance. In a short time, you will develop techniques that work best for you. Comparison shopping for a particular item, particularly if it's an expensive one, is valuable to serious negotiations.

Several years ago, I bought a guitar to satisfy my son's nagging--he was positive he was destined to become a rock star. Knowing the flightiness of teenage wants, I wasn't anxious to buy an expensive instrument, but I did want one with a good sound and decent quality. I spent the afternoon perusing any store that had guitars and 'talking' price. I closed the sale on a guitar for $25--the starting price was $125. The guitar, after many years of beach parties and get-togethers, still has one of the mellowest sounds I've ever heard.

On certain occasions, I do not bargain. If I feel the item is worth the price asked-- and a pair of enormous, brown eyes shyly peer up at me from behind Mama's well-worn skirt--I realize how much I have (even living on what I consider a shoestring existence) and gladly buy from this struggling merchant who undoubtedly provides for a family of six or more for a year on the same amount of money I require for a month's expenses.

If you are buying shoes or clothes, asking about size is not much help. Dresses and blouses are generally marked small, medium or large or assigned some mysterious, untranslatable series of numbers. The best way to assure a proper fit is to try it on. Many small clothing stores do not have dressing rooms and you must either hold it up and guess or try it on over your street clothes—and guess.

Besides goods that can be purchased in the downtown area, you will find vendors on every beach. I have won a few and lost a few on these deals. In Mazatlán, I bought a long, colorful print skirt with matching halter top for less than $10. From another 'salesman' I got a handsome woven rug for $10. At local stores, the dresses were a nonnegotiable $15 and a similar rug, $20. On the other hand, I bought a Mexican opal ring in a sterling silver setting for $6 from a seaside vendor in San Felipe. The identical ring in a jewelry store in Ensenada was $4.

On a Sunday, and sometimes Saturday, the flea markets bustle. <u>Everything</u> imaginable is for sale—or trade: used (well used) appliances, tires, tools, clothing, toys— you name it. Bargaining runs rampant. Do examine the merchandise: in some cases it's of poor quality, seconds or lower; sometimes it's damaged; frequently, there's nothing wrong. You must be the judge.

Another section I love to visit downtown is the plaza. Even small towns have these tree-shaded, flower bespeckled centers with benches that provide not only a place to rest weary bones out of the melting sun, but an area for listening to the infectious

beat of music pouring forth from mariachis
or wandering minstrels or to hear a visiting dignitary speak. During holidays, special activities are presented in the square.

Pushcart vendors surround the plazas of
larger towns. Peanuts, steamed clams and
oysters, gum, candy, corn on the cob, pop-
sicles, ice cream, soft drinks, 'carnitas,'
and fresh mixed fruits in a paper cup--it's
all quite a sight and the smells are most
tantalizing. Whether you buy and eat some
of these foods is a personal decision.

VOCABULARY

Where is____sold?
............¿DOHN-day say BEHN-day____?
          (¿Dónde se vende____?)
I want to buy____.
............Kee-AIR-oh kohm-PRAHR____.
          (Quiero comprar____.)
Where can I____?
................¿DOHN-day PWAY-doh____?
          (¿Dónde puedo____?)
How much is it?.........¿KWAHN-toh BAH-lay?
          (¿Cuánto vale?)
    or......................¿KWAHN-toh ehs?
          (¿Cuánto es?)
What size?..............¿Kay tah-MAH-nyoh?
          (¿Qué tamaño?)
What age? (for children)......¿Kay AH-nyoh?
          (¿Qué año?)
May I try this on?
............¿PWAY-doh proh-BAHR-may-loh?
          (¿Puedo probármelo?)
I like this one........May GOOS-tah EH-soh.
          (Me gusta eso.)
This is too expensive.
    EHS-toh ehs day-mah-see-AH-doh KAH-roh.
          (Ésto es demasiado caro.)

102

I will give you____pesos for it.
....Lay DOH-ee____PEH-sohs pohr EHS-toh.
     (Le doy____pesos por ésto.)
Something cheaper, please.
   AHL-goh mahs bah-RAH-toh, pohr fah-BOHR.
     (Algo más barato, por favor.)
I am just looking around.
   ...Ehs-TOY mee-RAHN-doh soh-loh-MEHN-tay.
     (Estoy mirando solomente.)
I will return____.........Boh-bay-RAY____.
          (Volveré____.)
Does it fit?.....................¿KAH-bay?
     (¿Cabe?)
It does not fit...............Noh KAH-bay.
          (No cabe.)
Here is your change (receipt).
   ....Ah-KEE tee-AY-nay soo KAHM-bee-oh
          (ray-SEE-boh).
     (Aquí tiene su cambio (recibo).
bargain sale.......BEHN-tah oh-kah-see-OHN
          (venta ocasión)
clearance sale
   .....BEHN-tah day lee-kwee-dah-see-OHN
          (venta de liquidación)
discount.....................dees-KWEHN-tah
             (discuenta)
receipt.......................ray-SEE-boh
          (recibo)
to refund................ray-ehm-bohl-SAHR
          (reembolsar)
sale............................BEHN-tah
          (venta)
   for sale...................day BEHN-tah
          (de venta)
   on sale....................ehn BEHN-tah
          (en venta)
sales tax
   ....eem-PWAYS-toh SOH-bray BEHN-tahs
          (impuesto sobre ventas)
souvenir.....................ray-KWEHR-doh
          (recuerdo)

PERSONAL ITEMS

alarm clock..............dehs-pehr-tah-DOHR
(despertador, m)
basket.........................kah-NAHS-tah
(canasta)
bathing suit..........TRAH-hay day BAH-nyoh
(traje (m) de baño)
belt..........................seen-too-ROHN
(cinturón, m)
blanket.......................frah-SAH-dah
(frazada)
   or..........................say-RAH-pay
(serape)
blouse...........................BLOO-sah
(blusa)
bracelet.......................pool-SAY-rah
(pulsera)
brassiére.......................SOHS-tehn
(sósten, m)
brush..........................say-PEE-yoh
(cepillo)
button...........................boh-TOHN
(botón, m)
cap.............................GOH-rrah
(gorra)
cloth..........................tay-HEE-doh
(tejido)
   or............................PAH-nyoh
(paño)
cotton......................ahl-goh-DOHN
(algodón, m)
embroidery.................bohr-DAH-dohs
(bordados)
kid.....................kah-bree-TEE-yah
(cabritilla)
lace..........................ehn-KAH-hay
(encaje, f)
leather.........................KWAY-roh
(cuero)
rayon............................ray-YOHN
(rayón, m)

```
silk........................SAY-dah
            (seda)
wool........................LAH-nah
            (lana)
comb........................PAY-nay
          (peine, m)
compact...............pohl-BAY-roh
          (polvero)
cuff links............hay-MAY-los
          (gemelos)
deodorant.........days-oh-doh-RAHN-tay
          (desodorante, m)
diaper....................pah-NYAHL
          (pañal, m)
dress..................behs-TEE-doh
          (vestido)
earring..........ehm-poo-nyee-DOO-rah
          (empuñidura)
  pair of earrings....pahr day ah-RAY-tays
          (par de aretes)
facial powder.........POHL-boh day KAH-rah
          (polvo de cara)
glasses, eye..............AHN-tay-OH-hohs
          (anteojos)
  or......................LEHN-tays
          (lentes, m)
  or......................GAH-fahs
          (gafas)
gloves...................GWAHN-tays
          (guantes)
guayabera...............gweye-yah-BAY-rah
(long sleeve shirt for men with two pockets
and darts down the front,  worn outside the
      pants, and  made in Yucatan)
handkerchief...............pah-nyoo-AY-loh
          (pañuelo)
hat.....................sohm-BRAY-roh
          (sombrero)
hose....................MAY-dee-ahs
          (medias)
  panty hose.........pahn-tee-MAY-dee-ahs
          (pantimedias)
```

housecoat............................BAH-tah
(bata)
jacket........................chah-MAH-rrah
(chamarra)
or........................chah-KAY-tah
(chaqueta)
jeans...........pahn-tah-LOH-nays day dreel
(pantalones de dril)
Kotex............................KOH-teks
(kotex, m)
lipstick.......peen-TOO-rah day LAH-bee^ohs
(pintura de labios)
nail polish.......peen-TOO-rah day OO-nyahs
(pintura de uñas)
necklace...........................koh-YAHR
(collar, m)
needle...........................ah-GOO-hah
(aguja)
pajamas.......................pee-HAH-mahs
(pijamas)
panties............................BRAH-gah
(braga)
or....................pahn-tah-LAY-tahs
(pantaletas)
pants....................pahn-tah-LOH-nays
(pantalones)
paper.............................pah-PEHL
(papel, m)
pen................................PLOO-mah
(pluma)
pendant...................pehn-dee^EHN-tay
(pendiente, m)
perfume..........................pahr-FOOM
(parfum, m)
or........................pehr-FOO-may
(perfume, m)
pins......................ahl-fee-LAY-rays
(alfileres)
purse.............................BOHL-sah
(bolsa)
raincoat..............eem-pehr-may^AH-blay
(impermeable)

```
razor.....................rahs-TREE-yoh
            (rastrillo)
   or.........MAH-kee-nah day ah-fay-TAHR
         (maquina de afeitar)
razor blade....koo-CHEE-yah day ah-fay-TAHR
         (cuchilla de afeitar)
ring.........................ah-NEE-yoh
            (anillo)
rouge............POHL-boh day kah-CHAY-tay
         (polvo de cachete)
safety pin..............eem-pehr-DEE-blay
            (imperdible)
sandals....................wah-RAH-chays
            (huaraches)
   or...................sahn-DAH-lee-ahs
            (sandalias)
sanitary belt
   .......seen-toor-OHN sah-nee-TAH-ree-oh
         (cinturón sanitario)
scarf.....................boo-FOON-dah
            (bufunda)
scissors...................tee-HAY-rahs
            (tijeras)
shampoo.......................chahm-POO
            (champú, m)
shaving cream.....hah-BOHN day rah-soo-RAHR
         (jabón (m) de rasurar)
shirt......................kah-MEE-sah
            (camisa)
shoe sole...................SWAY-lah
            (suela)
shoes......................sah-PAH-tohs
            (zapatos)
skirt......................FAHL-dah
            (falda)
slip.......................FOHN-doh
            (fondo)
socks..................kahl-say-TEE-nays
            (calcetines)
   or.......................MAY-dee-ahs
            (medias)
```

```
sun glasses...............GAH-fahs day sohl
              (gafas de sol)
sweater..........................SWAY-tehr
              (suéter, m)
sweatshirt........................MAH-yah
              (malla)
talcum powder.....................TAHL-koh
              (talco)
tampon...........................tah-POHN
              (tapón)
tennis shoes.....................TAY-nees
              (tenis)
thread.............................EE-loh
              (hilo)
tie..........................kohr-BAH-tah
              (corbata)
toilet paper.........pah-PEHL day BAH-nyoh
              (papel de baño)
tooth brush....say-PEE-yoh day dee⌃EHN-tays
              (cepillo de dientes)
tooth paste.......PAHS-tah day dee⌃EHN-tays
              (pasta de dientes)
underpants.......................TROO-sahs
              (trusas)
underwear, in general........kahl-SOH-nays
              (calzones, m)
   or..............ROH-pah een-tay-ree⌃OHR
              (ropa interior)
vest.........................chah-LAY-koh
              (chaleco)
wallet...................bee-yay-TAY-rah
              (billetera)
watch............................ray-LOH
              (reloj, m)
   wrist watch.....ray-LOH day pool-SAY-roh
              (reloj de pulsero)
zipper...................kray-mah-YAY-rah
              (cremallera)
```

CAMERAS

Go traveling without a camera? You have got to be kidding!

Mexican law states that you may take one still camera and one motion picture camera, either 8- or 16-millimeter, and a total of 12 rolls of film per person. Photographs must not be taken for commercial purposes and tripods are prohibited--I guess a tripod makes one fall into the professional category.

If you are like me, 12 rolls of film just will not hack it. On my last two week trip, I managed to shoot 256 photos...and this is someone who detests carrying cameras and taking photos.

So the inevitable happens--the search for a store that sells film. Film is available although it is more expensive than in the States.

VOCABULARY

Do you sell cameras here?
......¿Say BEHN-day KAH-mah-rahs ah-KEE?
      (¿Se vende cámaras aquí?)
What kind?.................¿Kay KLAH-sah?
            (¿Qué clase?)
Do you sell film?...........¿Eye ROH-yohs?
            (¿Hay rollos?)
Where can this film be developed?
.....¿DOHN-day say ray-BAY-lah ROH-yohs?
      (¿Dónde se revela rollos?)
I would like these films developed.
....Kee-see-AY-rah ray-bay-LAHR EHS-tahs
        FOH-tohs.
    (Quisiera revelar estas fotos.)

I need____film.

........Nay-say-SEE-toh ROH-yoh day____.
     (Necesito rollo de____.)

35MM
  TREHN-tah-ee-SEEN-koh mee-lee-MAY-troh
       (35 milimetro)

110.....................OO-noh dee⌃EHS
       (uno diez)

120....................OO-noh BEHN-tay
      (uno veinte)

127..........OO-noh behn-tee-see⌃AY-tay
     (uno veintisiete)

620......................sehs BEHN-tay
      (seis veinte)

Polaroid................poh-lah-ROHEED
      (polaroid)

black and white...BLAHN-koh ee NAY-groh
     (blanco y negro)

color.........................koh-LOHR
     (color, m)

Is it all right to take pictures?
    ....¿Say PWAY-day sah-KAHR FOH-tohs?
      (¿Se puede sacar fotos?)

Photographs are prohibited.
    ....Ehs-TAH proh-ee-BEE-doh toh-MAHR
       foh-toh-grah-FEE⌃ahs.
  (Está prohibido tomar fotografías.)

You may take pictures.
    ....Oos-TEHD PWAY-day sah-KAHR
       foh-toh-grah-FEE⌃ahs.
    (Ud. puede sacar fotografías.)

Can I take your picture?
    ....¿PWAY-day sah-KAHR soo FOH-toh.
      (¿Puede sacar su foto?)

camera lens......................LEHN-tay
      (lente, m)

¡Smile!....................¡Sohn-REE-sah!
      (¡Sonrisa!)

Say, cheese..............DEE-gah, KAY-soh.
     (Diga, queso.)

Um-m-m-m

If shopping is the "gravy" of traveling, then tasting excitingly different foods has to be the "potatoes." After 15 years of visiting Mexico, I still am discovering unusual or new foods. I have found only a few items that I will never buy or order again, so--

Try it! You probably will like it. A variety of delicious items with unusual seasonings and delectable combinations make dining a tasty, memorable experience. Because you may be unfamiliar with some of the foods, I have selected a few popular dishes and given a brief description.

black bean soup
.....SOH-pah day free-HOH-lays NAY-grohs
        (sopa de frijoles negros)
This hearty soup, popular in Puerto Rico,
is served with chopped onions on the side.
Delicious even on a hot day!

buñuelo......................boo-NUAY-loh
This dessert item is a deep-fried flour
tortilla, covered with sugar and cinnamon,
and served with butter. It always reminds
me of the way my mother used to fix left-
over pie dough.

burrito......................boo-RREE-toh
Is a soft, flour tortilla filled with
cheese, meat or chicken and covered with
sauce.

ceviche......................say-BEE-chay
Ceviche is uncooked, marinated white fish
with tomatoes, chili peppers, onions, sea-
sonings--and sometimes peas.

chile relleno.........CHEE-lay ray-YAY-noh
This is a green, Mexican chili whose seeds
and stem have been removed, then it's stuf-
fed with cheese, rolled in flour, a batter,
and fried.

chimichangas...........chee-mee-CHAHN-gahs
These are deep-fried burritos with a choice
of stuffings--chicken, beef or bean.

empanadas.................ehm-pah-NAH-dahs
Empanadas, meat pies, are flour tortillas
with meat sprinkled on one side, then fold-
ed in the middle and fried.

enchilada.................ehn-chee-LAH-dah
An enchilada is a tortilla rolled up with
cheese, beef or chicken inside, covered

with a cheese or tomato topping and baked
or simmered covered on top of the stove.

frijoles......................free-HOH-lays
Refried beans are served with breakfast,
lunch or dinner. The beans are placed in a
clay pot with water, covered and cooked
until soft and red then scooped into a fry-
ing pan with hot shortening, heated thoroughly and mashed.

gazpacho.....................gahs-PAH-choh
This spicy tomato-based soup is served re-
freshingly cold.

guacamole..................gwah-kah-MOH-lay
Made from avocados, guacamole has chopped
onions, tomatoes, chili peppers and tabasco
added to give a savory flavor. It can be
served with fried tortilla chips as a dip
or over the top of foods as a sauce.

menudo.........................may-NOO-doh
This soup is made from whole corn kernels
and bits and pieces of beef that we consider inedible. Perhaps, we should take
note because the end result is an excellent
tasting soup.

pozole.........................poh-SOH-lay
Pozole is soup made from large kernels of
corn, flavored with pork and served with a
variety of additions--radish, onion, cab-
bage, hot sauce and more.

quesadillas................kay-sah-DEE-yahs
These are large, flour tortillas with
cheese on top that are frequently served as
appetizers.

sopa and caldo............SOH-pah, KAHL-doh
Two words, sopa and caldo, both mean soup

and are frequently interchangeable. Generally, sopa is used for thick soups like stew and spaghetti dishes while caldo refers to thinner soups or broths.

taco..................................TAH-koh
A taco is a golden tortilla with cheese, beans, chicken or meat inside. In the States, the meat is usually hamburger but in Mexico, the beef is toasted or boiled and frequently is stringy in texture.

tamales.......................tah-MAH-lays
Tamales are corn husks filled with cooked meat, chili peppers, vegetables, olives and seasonings then tied shut. Water is added to the bottom of a large pot and the tamales steamed until the potatoes are done.

torta..............................TOHR-tah
A torta is similar to a submarine sandwich and is made from a birote or bolillo. (See, BREADS, page 121 for details.) Innumerable edibles are tucked inside.

tortilla.....................tohr-TEE-yah
Corn tortillas are a staple in the Mexican diet. The difference between store purchased tortillas and the ones you make is the flour. The tortillas you purchase in a tortillería are made from raw kernels of corn, cooked in a lime solution, then mashed wet. The corn flour you buy is milled dry which causes the color and taste difference.

Flour tortillas are usually larger than corn ones. Many Americans like them better than those of corn because when flattened and cooked over a griddle, they taste somewhat like unsweetened pie dough.

In Spain, a tortilla is entirely different:
it's an omelette. There are tortillas of
potatoes, ham or anything that combines
well with eggs.

tostado......................tohs-TAH-doh
This is a hard-fried tortilla usually covered with refried beans. There are chicken,
beef or pork tostados. All are garnished
with lettuce, tomatoes, hot sauce and
cheese.

VOCABULARY

Where is a good restaurant?...¿DOHN-day eye
....oon bwehn rehs-tahoo-RAHN-tay?
(¿Dónde hay un buen restaurante?)
A table for four, please.
.......OO-nah MAY-sah PAH-rah KWAH-troh,
pohr fah-BOHR.
(Una mesa para cuatro, por favor.)
What do you recommend?
¿Kay nohs ray-koh-mee͡EHN-dah oos-TEHD?
(¿Qué nos recomienda ud.?)
I want to order____.
............Kee͡AIR-oh ohr-day-NAHR____.
(Quiero ordenar____.)
Please bring me____.
..........Fah-BOHR day trah͡EHR-may____.
(Favor de traerme____.)
I would like____........Kee-see͡AY-rah____.
(Quisiera____.)
.....two orders of this and one of that.
dohs OHR-day-nays day EHS-tay ee OO-noh
day EH-say.
(...dos ordenes de éste y uno de ése.)
I like my meat (rare, etc., pages 117,118)
............Kee͡AIR-oh lah-KAHR-nay____.
(Quiero la carne____.)
More____, please...Mahs____, pohr fah-BOHR.
(Más____, por favor.

115

Is the tip included?
¿Ehs-TAH een-kloo-EE-dah lah proh-PEE-nah?
    (Está incluída la propina?)

I need a___ ....Nay-say-SEE-toh oon___ .
         (Necesito un (-a)___ .)
  ash tray...............say-nee-SAY-roh
            (cenicero)
  bowl...................ehs-koo-DEE-yah
            (escudilla)
  clean table cloth..mahn-TEHL LEEM-pee-oh
         (mantel (m) limpio)
  cup............................TAH-sah
            (taza)
  fork.......................tay-nay-DOHR
            (tenedor, m)
  glass...........................BAH-soh
            (vaso)
    wine glass...............bah-SEE-toh
            (vasito)
  knife.....................koo-CHEE-yoh
            (cuchillo)
  napkin.................sehr-bee-YAY-tah
            (servilleta)
  plate........................PLAH-toh
            (plato)
  salt shaker................sah-LAY-roh
            (salero)
  saucer....................plah-TEE-yoh
            (platillo)
  seasonings............see pages 132-136
  soup bowl...............PLAH-toh OHN-doh
            (plato hondo)
  spoon.....................koo-CHAH-rah
            (cuchara)

cashier.......................kah-HAY-roh
            (cajero)
change.........................FAY-ree-ah
            (feria)
check...........................KWEHN-tah
            (cuenta)

116

```
menu.............................LEES-tah
                (lista)
restaurant.............rehs-tahoo-RAHN-tay
            (restaurante, m)
tip..........................proh-PEE-nah
                (propina)
waiter........................may-SAY-roh
                (mesero)
waitress......................may-SAY-rah
                (mesera)
wine list.............LEES-tah day BEE-noh
            (lista de vino)
```

COOKING METHODS

```
baked.......................ohr-nay-AH-doh
                (horneado)
breaded................ehm-pah-nee-SAH-doh
                (empanizado)
broiled........................ah-SAH-doh
                (asado)
charcoal broiled.............ahl kahr-BOHN
                (al carbón)
fried...........................FREE-toh
                (frito)
grilled......................pah-RREE-yah
                (parrilla)
mashed..........................poo-RAY
                (purée)
medium.....................may-dee-AH-noh
                (mediano)
preparada................pray-pah-RAH-dah
  (Indicates whatever it is has been cooked
  according to how the cook wanted to fix
  it. This can change within the same
  restaurant from day to day.)
rare...................ah lah een-GLAY-sah
            (a la inglesa)
roasted.......................ah-SAH-doh
                (asado)
toasted......................tohs-TAH-doh
                (tostado)
```

```
well done..............ah lah ehs-pah-NYOHL
              (a la español)
eggs (ways of cooking).............WAY-bohs
              (huevos)
   hard boiled........bee⌃EHN koh-SEE-dohs
              (bien cocidos)
   fried.........................FREE-tohs
              (fritos)
   over easy..........ray-bohl-tay⌃AH-dohs
              (revolteados)
   poached....................ehr-BEE-dohs
              (hervidos)
   ranch style..............rahn-CHAY-rohs
              (rancheros)
   scrambled................ray-BWEHL-tohs
              (revueltos)
   soft boiled.................TEE-bee⌃ohs
              (tibios)
   up....................ehs-tray-YAH-dohs
              (estrellados)
```

ON THE MENU

```
afternoon special..koh-MEE-dah koh-RREE-dah
              (comida corrida)
a la mode...................ah lah MOH-dah
              (a la moda)
apertif....................ah-pehr-TEE-boh
              (apertivo)
bacon and eggs....toh-SEE-nah kohn WAY-bohs
              (tocina con huevos)
bread (see BREADS, page 121)..........pahn
              (pan, m)
breakfast..................day-sah-YOO-noh
              (desayuno)
cake.............................pahs-TEHL
              (pastel, m)
   or.............................TOHR-tah
              (torta)
chicken (see POULTRY, pages 122-123)POH-yoh
              (pollo)
```

118

```
cocktail (drink or shrimp)........kohk-TEHL
              (coctél, m)
corn flakes....................my-SOH-roh
              (maisoro)
cracker........................gah-YAY-tah
              (galleta)
cream of wheat................kray-MOH-lah
              (cremola)
custard (my favorite)................flahn
              (flan, m)
dessert........................POHS-tray
              (postre, m)
dinner..........................SAY-nah
              (cena)
drinks (see BEVERAGES, pages 124-125)
..........................bay-BEE-dahs
              (bebidas)
flapjack.....................oh-WHAY-lah
              (hojuela)
French fries............PAH-pahs FREE-tahs
              (papas fritas)
fruit (see FRUITS, pages 128-129)..FROO-tah
              (fruta)
hamburger................ahm-boor-GAY-sah
              (hamburgesa)
hot sauce............SAHL-sah pee-KAHN-tay
              (salsa piquante)
ice cream......................ay-LAH-doh
              (helado)
jello.........................HAY-yoh
              (jello)
jelly or jam..............mehr-may-LAH-dah
              (mermelada)
juice.........................HOO-goh
              (jugo)
lunch....................ahl-moo-AIR-soh
              (almuerzo)
   or.........................koh-MEE-dah
              (comida)
milk (see DAIRY PRODUCTS, pages 121-122)
..............................LAY-chay
              (leche, f)
```

meat (see MEATS, pages 122-123)....KAHR-nay
                    (carne, f)
melon............................may-LOHN
                    (melón)
oatmeal.........................ah-BAY-nah
                    (avena)
omelette.........tohr-TEE-yah day WAY-bohs
            (tortilla de huevos)
orange juice, rolls and coffee
...............WHO-goh day nah-RAH-hah,
        pah-nay-SEE-yohs, ee kah-FAY
    (jugo de naranja, panecillos, y café)
pancakes........................pahn-KAYKS
                    (los pancakes)
potato chips.............PAH-pahs FREE-tahs
                    (papas fritas)
pudding.........................poo-DEEN
                    (pudín, m)
ribs........................kohs-TEE-yahs
                    (costillas)
salad.......................ehn-sah-LAH-dah
                    (ensalada)
sandwich......................SAHND-weech
                    (sandwich, m)
seafood......................mah-REES-kohs
                    (mariscos)
    (for all fish and shellfish, see
                pages 154-157)
sherbet.......................nee-AY-bay
                    (nieve, f)
    or........................sohr-BAY-tay
                    (sorbete, m)
soup............................SOH-pah
                    (sopa)
    or...........................KAHL-doh
                    (caldo)
toast....................pahn tohs-TAH-doh
                    (pan tostado)
vegetables (see VEGETABLES, pages 129-131)
........................behr-DOO-rahs
                    (verduras)

BREADS

Mexican breads are much sweeter than ours. They are more like dessert rolls and, even though the shapes differ, they all seem to taste the same.

birote.........................bee-ROH-tay
bolillo........................boh-LEE-yoh
These two bread types are interchangeable and are made of the basic sweet-bread dough. The equivalent of our submarine sandwich is created using either of them.

semita.........................say-MEE-tah
A semita looks like a hamburger bun but once again is sweeter. It really doesn't make a good substitute for the real thing.

Bimbo...........................BEEM-boh
If you are restocking your provisions, ask for "Bimbo" which is the name of a commercially baked bread--like ours.

Don't forget to include tortillas as a substitute for bread. Spread them with butter and serve with dinner or coat them with peanut butter, sprinkle with fresh alfalfa sprouts, and roll them up for a tasty snack.

DAIRY PRODUCTS

butter....................mahn-tay-KEE-yah
                  (mantequilla)
cheese...........................KAY-soh
                  (queso)
   white cheese..........KAY-soh BLAHN-koh
            (queso blanco)
   yellow cheese.....KAY-soh ah-mah-REE-yoh
            (queso amarillo)

cottage cheese.................ray-kay-SOHN
(requesón, m)
cream.............................KRAY-mah
(crema)
eggs..............................WAY-bohs
(huevos)
    eggs, powdered.....WAY-bohs ehn POHL-boh
            (huevos en polvo)
margarine..................mahr-gah-REE-nah
(margarina)
milk..............................LAY-chay
(leche, f)
    powdered milk......LAY-chay ehn POHL-boh
            (leche en polvo)
    Alpura.......................ahl-POO-rah
    (A sterilized milk that keeps, unopened,
    at room temperature for three months.
    Refrigerate after opening.)

MEATS AND POULTRY

(For fish, seafood, see pages 154-157)

armadillo..................ahr-mah-DEE-yoh
bacon.........................toh-SEE-nah
(tocina)
beef...................................rays
(res, f)
beef steak.......................BEEF-tehk
(biftec)
burro.............................BOO-rroh
chicken...........................POH-yoh
(pollo)
deer...........................bay-NAH-doh
(venado)
duck..............................PAH-toh
(pato)
goat.............................CHEE-boh
(chivo)
    on the menu, it's..............KAH-brah
            (cabra)

122

young goat..................chee-BEE-toh
(chivito)

ham................................hah-MOHN
(jamón, m)

iguana........................ee-GWAH-nah

hamburger..................ahm-boor-GAY-sah
(hamburguesa)

hare..........................lee-AY-bray
(liebre, f)

hot dog............PAY-rroh kah-lee-EHN-tay
(perro caliente)

    or......................sahl-CHEE-chah
(salchicha)

lamb..........................kohr-DAY-roh
(cordero)

    or......................kahr-NAY-roh
(carnero)

    wild ones..................boh-RRAY-goh
(borrego)

lamb chops...choo-LAY-tahs day kahr-NAY-roh
(chuletas de carnero)

meat..............................KAHR-nay
(carne, f)

    grated and dried...........mah-CHAH-kah
(machaca)

    ground.............KAHR-nay moh-LEE-dah
(carne molida)

pork..............................PWEHR-koh
(puerco)

pork sausage..................choh-REE-soh
(chorizo)

rabbit..........................koh-NAY-hoh
(conejo)

sirloin....................soh-loh-MEE-yoh
(solomillo)

    or.......................soh-LOH-moh
(solomo)

snake..........................koo-LAY-brah
(culebra)

turkey...........................PAH-boh
(pavo)

BEVERAGES

```
beverages.....................bay-BEE-dahs
                (bebidas)
hot chocolate.............choh-koh-LAH-tay
             (chocolate, m)
coffee...........................kah-FAY
                (café, m)
   black...........................SOH-loh
                (solo)
   with sugar.............kohn ah-SOO-kahr
                (con azúcar)
   with cream................kohn KRAY-mah
                (con crema)
   1/2 coffee, 1/2 milk.......kohn LAY-chay
                (con leche)
ice tea.....................tay ay-LAH-doh
                (té helado)
juice, fruit.................WHO-goh de____
                (jugo de____)
lemonade...................lee-moh-NAH-dah
                (limonada)
milk............................LAY-chay
                (leche, f)
milkshake.....................bah-TEE-doh
                (batido)
soft drink...................ray-FREHS-koh
                (refresco)
tea................................tay
                (té, m)
```

TYPES OF ALCOHOLIC BEVERAGES

```
alcohol..........................ahl-KOHL
                (alcól, m)
   aged..........................ah-NAY-hoh
                (anejo)
beer.........................sehr-BAY-sah
                (cerveza)
brandy..........................BRAHN-dee
                (brandi, m)
```

124

```
champagne...................chahm-PAH-nyah
                (champaña)
Cointreau......................kohn-TROY
                (controy, m)
cognac.........................KOHN-yahk
                (coñac)
gin..........................hee-NAY-brah
                (ginebra)
Kahlua.......................kah-LOO-ah
liqueur (any fruit)........lee-KOHR day____
                (licor de____)
rum................................rohn
                (ron, m)
Rompope.......................rohm-POH-pay
   (Made in Mexico, tastes something like a
   Christmas eggnog mix. Excellent over
   chocolate ice cream or canned mangos.)
Scotch...............WEES-kee ehs-koh-SAYS
            (whisky escocés)
sherry..........................hay-REHS
                (jeréz, m)
tequila.......................tay-KEE-lah
vodka...........................BOHD-kah
                (vodka)
whiskey.........................WEES-kee
                (whisky)
wine.............................BEE-noh
                (vino)
   claret.............BEE-noh klah-RAY-tay
            (vino clarete)
   cream sherry...........hay-REHS DOOL-say
            (jeréz dulce)
   red............................ROH-soh
                (roso)
   or..........................TEEN-toh
                (tinto)
   sauterne or white......BEE-noh BLAHN-koh
            (vino blanco)
   with a lime.............kohn LEE-mah
                (con lima)
   with a lemon.............kohn lee-MOHN
                (con limón)
```

MIXES

```
7 UP..........................SAY-behn op
Coca Cola..................KOH-kah KOH-lah
water............................AH-gwah
                (agua, m)
    carbonated....................kohn gahs
                (con gas)
      or.................kohn boor-BOO-hahs
              (con burbujas)
    distilled.......AH-gwah days-tee-LAH-dah
              (aqua destilada)
    drinking...........AH-gwah poh-TAH-blay
              (agua potable)
    filtered (DO NOT DRINK)
              ..............AH-gwah feel-TRAH-dah
              (agua filtrada)
    mineral............AH-gwah mee-nay-RAHL
              (agua de mineral)
    plain..........seen gahs (boor-BOO-hahs)
            (sin gas, (burbujas)
    soda................AH-gwah kohn SOH-dah
              (agua con soda)
tonic.........................TOH-nee-koh
                (tónico)
on the rocks (Be careful!).....kohn YAY-loh
              (con hielo)
```

FRUITS AND VEGETABLES

You will run across some unusual fruits and vegetables that are unfamiliar to you. Some you may like, some you may not.

chayote........................chah-YOH-tay
The chayote is a small squash that has a thorny skin. Cook it before eating.

guayaba........................gwah-YAH-bah
A guayaba is a green to yellow fruit with a most unique taste--you will like it or hate it. Eat the whole thing, seeds and all.

jícama.........................HEE-kah-mah
The jícama has a mild turnip flavor and is fleshy and sweet. Peel it and eat it raw. It is low in calories and a good substitute for water chestnuts. Serve it in a mixed fruit salad or dessert or alone, partially covered with orange juice. The Mexicans sprinkle it with chili powder.

mangos.........................MAHN-gohs
Mangos are frequently garnished with lime or lemon slices. When eaten green, they have a tangy-taste; when ripe, they are extremely sweet.

papaya.........................pah-PAH-yah
Like the mango, this is sweet, nourishing and served with a citrus slice.

pitahaya.......................pee-tah-AH-yah
A pitahaya has a texture similar to watermelon and is the semi-sweet fruit of a cactus.

quenepas.......................kay-NAY-pahs
Quenepas, found in Puerto Rico, come in bunches and are sold by pushcart vendors.

It is a small, greenish fruit with a large seed--don't eat the seed.

tuna................................TOO-nah
The tuna is the fruit of what we know as the prickly pear cactus. Once you get past the thorns, it's quite good.

FRUITS

apple..........................mahn-SAH-nah
                (manzana)
apricot....................chah-bah-KAH-noh
                (chabacano)
avocado....................ah-gwah-KAH-tay
                (aguacate, m)
banana.......................PLAH-tah-noh
                (plátano)
  or.......................bah-NAH-nah
                (banana)
cantalope.......................may-LOHN
                (melón, m)
cassava......................kah-SAH-bay
                (cazabe, m)
cherry........................say-RAY-sah
                (cereza)
citrus........................SEE-tree-koh
                (cítrico)
coconut..........................KOH-koh
                (coco)
date............................DAH-teel
                (dátil, m)
fig...............................EE-goh
                (higo)
fruit...........................FROO-tah
                (fruta)
grape............................OO-bah
                (uva)
grapefruit....................toh-ROHN-hah
                (toronja)
lemon...........................lee-MOHN
                (limón, m)

```
lime................................LEE-mah
                  (lima)
mango..............................MAHN-goh
                  (mango)
olive........................ah-say-TOO-nah
                  (aceituna)
orange.......................nah-RAHN-hah
                  (naranja)
peach........................doo-RAHS-noh
                  (durazno)
pear..............................PAY-rah
                  (pera)
pineapple..........................PEE-nyah
                  (piña)
plum (or prune)..............see-roo-AY-lah
                  (ciruela)
pomegranate....................grah-NAH-dah
                  (granada)
pumpkin....................kah-lah-BAY-sah
                  (calabeza)
raisin.............................PAH-sah
                  (pasa)
strawberry........................FRAY-sah
                  (fresa)
tangerine..................tahn-hay-REE-nah
                  (tangerina)
tomato.........................toh-MAH-tay
                  (tomate, m)
watermelon......................sahn-DEE-ah
                  (sandía)
```

VEGETABLES

```
artichoke..................ahl-kah-CHOH-fah
                  (alcachofa)
asparagus..................ehs-PAH-rrah-goh
                  (espárrago)
beans........................free-HOH-lays
                  (frijoles, m)
   or................................AH-bah
                  (haba)
```

129

```
    black........free-HOH-lays NAY-grohs
           (frijoles negros)
    string................ay-HOH-tay
           (ejote, m)
    green.........hoo-DEE^ahs BEHR-days
           (judías verdes)
beets.....................bay-tah-BAY-lays
           (betabeles, f)
broccoli........................BRAY-kohl
           (brécol, m)
Brussels sprouts.............bray-TOH-nays
           (bretones, m)
cabbage.............................kohl
              (col, f)
    or........................ray-POH-yoh
              (repollo)
carrot..................sah-nah-OHR-ee^ah
              (zanahoria)
cauliflower..................koh-lee-FLOHR
              (coliflor, m)
celery..........................AH-pee^oh
              (apio)
corn on the cob.................ay-LOH-tay
              (elote, m)
    off and dried....................mah^EES
              (maíz, m)
    sweet...............mah^EES tee^EHR-noh
              (maíz tierno)
cucumber........................pay-PEE-noh
              (pepino)
    or.........................koh-OHM-broh
              (cohombro)
eggplant..................bay-rehn-HAY-nah
              (berenjena)
garbanzos....................gahr-BAHN-sohs
garlic...............................AH-hoh
              (ajo)
lettuce......................lay-CHOO-gah
              (lechuga)
Lima bean................AH-bah de LEE-mah
              (haba de Lima)
```

```
mushroom..........................OHN-goh
                (hongo)
    or.............................SAY-tah
                (seta)
onion.........................say-BOH-yah
                (cebolla)
pea.........................ghee-SAHN-tay
                (guisante, m)
peas......................CHEE-chah-rohs
                (chícharos)
peppers, green or red.............CHEE-lay
                (chile, m)
potato...........................PAH-pah
                (papa)
potato, sweet (yam)............kah-MOH-tay
                (camote, m)
    or.........................bah-TAH-tah
                (batata)
radish........................RAH-bah-noh
                (rábano)
rice.............................ah-RROHS
                (arroz, m)
spinach....................ehs-pee-NAH-kah
                (espinaca)
squash....................kah-lah-BAH-sah
                (calabaza)
Swiss chard....................ah-SEHL-gah
                (acelga)
turnip...........................NAH-boh
                (nabo)
vegetable....................lay-GOOM-bray
                (legumbre, f)
    or.......................bay-hay-TAHL
                (vegetal, m)
vegetables...................behr-DOO-rahs
                (verduras)
zucchini..............kah-lah-bah-SEE-tahs
                (calabazitas)
```

AT THE MARKET

If you want a fruit or vegetable in a can,
say the noun and follow it with:
    ....ehn LAH-tah
             (en lata)
For foods in a bottle, like a jar:
    ....ehn FRAHS-koh
             (en frasco)
Bottled soft drinks:
    ....ehn boh-TAY-yah
             (en botella)
  in a box....................ehn KAH-hah
             (en caja)
  in a sack...................ehn SAH-koh
             (en saco)
no return (bottle).........noh ray-TOOR-noh
             (no returno)
no deposit..............noh day-POH-see-toh
             (no depósito)
label...........................MAHR-koh
             (marco)

STAPLES AND SEASONINGS

almond.....................ahl-MEHN-drah
             (almendra)
aluminum foil.....pah-PEHL day ehs-TAH-nyoh
          (papel de estaño)
baking powder..lay-bah-DOO-rah ehn POHL-boh
        (levadura en polvo)
baking soda
        bee-kahr-boh-NAH-toh day SOH-sah
         (bicarbonato de sosa)
barley......................say-BAH-dah
             (cebada)
basil.....................ahl-bah-AH-kah
            (albahaca, m)
Bimbo.........................BEEM-boh
      (commercially baked bread)
bleach....................blahn-kay-AHR
            (blanquear)

bread............................pahn
               (pan, m)
buckwheat (cereal)............ahl-fohr-FOHN
            (alforfón, m)
buckwheat flour
           ah-REE-nah day ahl-fohr-FOHN
        (harina de alforfón)
catsup..........................KAHT-soop
            (catsup, m)
cereal........................say-ray-AHL
            (cereal, m)
   or..........................GRAH-noh
            (grano)
chlorine........................KLOH-roh
            (cloro)
chocolate................choh-koh-LAH-tay
          (chocolate, m)
cigar...........................POO-roh
            (puro)
cigarettes...................see-GAH-rrohs
           (cigarros)
   or.....................see-gah-REE-yohs
           (cigarillos)
cinnamon......................kah-NAY-lah
           (canela)
cleanser..................leem-pee-ah-DOHR
          (limpiador)
clove...........................KLAH-boh
           (clavo)
cocoa.......................koh-KAH-oh
           (cocao)
coffee..........................kah-FAY
           (café, m)
cookie......................gah-YAY-tah
           (galleta)
corn flakes...................my-SOH-roh
           (maizoro)
corn husks, package of
          mah-NOH-hoh day OH-hahs
        (manojo de hojas)
cream of wheat...............kray-MOH-lah
           (cremola)

```
detergent.................day-tehr-HEHN-tay
              (detergente, m)
drinks, soft.............ray-FREHS-kohs
              (refrescos)
eggs, a dozen.......doh-SAY-nah de WAY-bohs
              (docena de huevos)
flour, wheat..................ah-REE-nah
              (harina)
   corn.......................mah-SAY-kah
              (maseca)
garlic...........................AH-hoh
              (ajo)
gelatine.................hay-lah-TEE-nah
              (gelatina)
ginger.....................hehn-HEE-bray
              (jengibre, m)
gum...........................CHEE-klay
              (chicle, m)
   bubble gum........CHEE-klay day bah-LOHN
              (chicle de balón)
herb...........................YEHR-bah
              (hierba)
honey...........................mee^EHL
              (miel, m)
jam, marmalade............mehr-may-LAH-dah
              (mermelada)
jelly.........................hah-LAY^ah
              (jalea)
lard.........................mahn-TAY-kah
              (manteca)
liquor........................lee-KOHR
              (licor, m)
marshmallow............mahl-bah-BEES-kohs
              (malvaviscos)
match.......................say-REE-yoh
              (cerillo)
   or........................FOHS-foh-roh
              (fósforo)
mayonnaise...............mah-yoh-NAY-sah
              (mayonesa)
mousetrap................rah-toh-NAY-rah
              (ratonera)
```

```
mustard.....................mohs-TAH-sah
               (mostaza)
napkins.................sehr-bee-YAY-tahs
               (servilletas)
noodle......................tah-yah-REEN
               (tallarín)
nut..............................noo-EHS
               (nuez, f)
nutmeg..............noo-EHS mohs-KAH-dah
               (nuez moscada)
oats, oatmeal...................ah-BAY-nah
               (avena)
oil (cooking, salad, or car)
  ...........................ah-SAY-tay
               (aceite, m)
olive oil........ah-SAY-tay day oh-LEE-bah
               (aceite de oliva)
oregano....................oh-RAY-gah-noh
               (orégano)
paprika.....................pee-mehn-TOHN
               (pimentón, m)
paraffin...................pah-rah-FEE-nah
               (parafina)
parsley.......................pay-ray-HEEL
               (perejil, m)
peanut......................kah-kah-WAY-tay
               (cacahuete, m)
peanut butter..KRAY-mah day kah-kah-WAY-tay
           (crema de cacahuete)
pecan........................pah-KAH-nah
               (pacana)
pepper.....................pee-mee-EHN-tah
               (pimienta)
peppercorn.....GRAH-noh day pee-mee-EHN-tah
           (grano de pimienta)
pickle.....................ehn-koor-TEE-doh
               (encurtido)
popcorn......................roh-SAY-tahs
               (rosetas)
rice............................ah-RROHS
               (arroz, m)
```

```
saffron......................ah-sah-FRAHN
              (azafrán, m)
salad dressing................ah-LEE-nyoh
              (aliño)
salt................................sahl
              (sal, m)
sauce...........................SAHL-sah
              (salsa)
   hot sauce..........SAHL-sah pee-KAHN-tay
              (salsa picante)
soap............................hah-BOHN
              (jabón, m)
spice........................ehs-PAY-see-ah
              (especia)
sugar..........................ah-SOO-kahr
              (azúcar, m)
syrup..........................hah-RAH-bay
              (jarabe, m)
tabasco......................tah-BAHS-koh
tea.................................tay
              (té, m)
toilet paper..........pah-PEHL day BAH-nyoh
          (papel (m) de baño)
vanilla........................buy-NEE-yah
              (vainilla)
vinegar......................bee-NAH-gray
              (vinagre, m)
wax paper......pah-PEHL day ehn-say-RAH-doh
          (papel de encerado)
wheat..............................TREE-goh
              (trigo)
```

COOKING UTENSILS

```
baking pan.............MOHL-day day OHR-noh
          (molde (m) de horno)
blender......................lee-kwah-DOHR
              (liquador, m)
bota................................BOH-tah
          (small leather wine bag)
botijo........................boh-TEE-hoh
          (a clay water jug)
```

```
bottle opener..........AH-bray boh-TAY-yahs
              (abre botellas)
bowl....................ehs-koo-DEE-yah
              (escudilla)
   or.........................bahn-DAY-hah
              (bandeja)
can opener...............AH-bray-LAH-tahs
              (abrelatas)
chocolate beater............bah-tee-DOH-rah
              (batidora)
coffeepot..................kah-fay-TAY-rah
              (cafetera)
colander......................koh-lah-DOHR
              (colador, m)
corkscrew..................tee-rah-boo-SOHN
              (tirabuzón, f)
corn tortilla press..............PREHN-sah
              (prensa)
dishes, set of..................bah-HEE-yah
              (vajilla)
frying pan.......................sahr-TEHN
              (sartén)
griddle...........................koh-MAHL
              (comal, m)
lid...............................TAH-pah
              (tapa)
mixing bowl...................bahn-DAY-hah
              (bandeja)
pot...............................OH-yah
              (olla)
pressure cooker.....OH-yah day pray-see-OHN
              (olla de preción)
saucepan...................kah-say-ROH-lah
              (caserola)
serving spoon................koo-chah-ROHN
              (cucharón, m)
spatula....................ehs-PAH-too-lah
              (espátula)
tamale pot.................OH-yah GRAHN-day
              (olla grande)
tea kettle....................mahr-MEE-tah
              (marmita)
```

A night in a hotel or motel (especially if
you have come by boat with limited or no
extra fresh water for showers) is a pleasant change of pace. Once you arrive at the
larger city, "shop around" a bit and you
can find adequate rooms priced reasonably
--if you do not stay in the big American
hotels that can cost upwards from $100 per
night.

In Puerto Vallarta, one of the more expensive areas, we found a clean, nicely-kept hotel, one block from the beach and a few blocks from the shopping area for $20 per night. I talked to another American who had found a cottage, right on the beach, for $18 per night.

I am referring to larger towns some distance from the States. If you are going to Ensenada for a weekend during the tourist season, you better have reservations. There simply are not enough accommodations to handle the numbers that bombard this popular near-to-the-border town.

Beware the tap water. An uncomfortable mistake I made while in Acapulco was to nonchalantly brush my teeth with water from the faucet. I suffered for the next week from this thoughtless deed.

VOCABULARY

My name is____ ....May YAH-moh____ .
    (Me llamo____ .)
I have reservations.
  .....TEHN-goh ray-sehr-bah-see‿OHN-ays.
    (Tengo reservaciones.)
Do you have a room?........¿Eye KWAHR-tohs?
    (¿Hay cuartos?)
There are____ in our party.....SOH-mohs____ .
    (Somos____ .)
____children and___ adults.
   ____NEE-nyohs ee____ah-DOOL-tohs.
  (____niños y____adultos.)

I want two connecting rooms.
  ....Kee‿AIR-oh dohs KWAHR-tohs
    koh-moo-nee-KAH-dohs.
  (Quiero dos cuartos comunicados.)

I want a room with:
..........Kee-AIR-oh oon KWAHR-toh kohn:
    (Quiero un cuarto con____.)
a double bed
        ...KAH-mah mah-tree-mohn-ee-AHL
        (cama matrimonial)
single beds
    ....KAH-mahs een-dee-bee-doo-AH-lays
        (camas individuales)
a bath....................oon BAH-nyoh
                (un baño)
a toilet.............oon ehs-koo-SAH-doh
                (un escusado)
a shower................OO-nah DOO-chah
                (una ducha)
hot water........AH-gwah kahl-ee-EHN-tay
            (agua caliente)

How much is it____?.....¿KWAHN-toh ehs____?
                (¿Cuánto es____?)
per night.................pohr NOH-chay
                (por noche)
per week...............pohr say-MAH-nah
                (por semana)
per month....................pohr mehs
                (por mes)

Are the meals included?
............¿Ehs-TAHN lahs koh-MEE-dahs
            een-kloo-EE-dahs?
    (¿Están las comidas incluídas?)
Do you accept checks in payment?
.........¿Ah-SEHP-tah oos-TEHD CHAY-kays
            ehn PAH-goh?
    (¿Acepta ud. cheques en pago?)
We are leaving____.......Pahr-TEE-mohs____.
        (Partimos____.)
We are staying several days.
........Nohs kay-DAH-mohs ah-KEE OO-nohs
            POH-kohs DEE-ahs.
    (Nos quedamos aquí unos pocos días.)

140

```
        ...only tonight.
        ......soh-lah-MEHN-tay EHS-tah NOH-chay.
              (solamente esta noche.)
Can I see the room?.....¿PWAY-doh BEHR-loh?
                (¿Puedo verlo?)
This room is too____.
  EHS-tay KWAHR-toh ehs day-mah-see-AH-doh_.
      (Este cuarto es demasiado____.)


    small....................pay-KAY-nyoh
                  (pequeño)
    noisy...................roo-ee-DOH-soh
                  (ruidoso)
    hot.....................kah-lee-EHN-tay
                  (caliente)
    cold..........................FREE-oh
                  (frío)
It has no view.
      .......Noh tee-EH-nay BWAY-nah BEES-tah.
            (No tiene buena vista.)
Call me at____.....YAH-may-may ah lahs____.
            (Llámeme a las____.)
Wake me at____.
      .......Dehs-pee-EHR-tay-may ah lahs____.
            (Despiértame a las____.)
The____does not work......Noh SEER-bay____.
                (No sirve____.)
How much do I owe you?..¿KWAHN-toh DAY-boh?
                (¿Cuánto debo?)
Where shall I leave the keys?
        ........¿DOHN-day DAY-hoh lahs YAH-bays?
            (¿Dónde dejo las llaves?)


Bring____.....................TRY-gah____.
                (Traiga____.)
    blanket........................MAHN-tah
                    (manta)
    pillowcase...FOON-dah day ahl-moh-AH-dah
            (funda de almohada)
    sheet.......................SAH-bah-nah
                    (sábana)
```

```
soap..........................hah-BOHN
            (jabón, m)
toilet paper..pah-PEHL ee-hee-EH-nee-koh
            (papel higiénico)
or................pah-PEHL day BAH-nyoh
            (papel de baño)
towels......................toh-AH-yahs
            (toallas)
wash cloths........toh-AH-yahs CHEE-kahs
            (toallas chicas)


bell hop...................kah-mah-RAY-roh
            (camarero)
front room.........KWAHR-toh ahl FREHN-tay
            (cuarto al frente)
   back.............KWAHR-toh ahl FOHN-doh
            (cuarto al fondo)
   quiet...........KWAHR-toh trahn-KEE-loh
            (cuarto tranquilo)
lower floor................PEE-soh BAH-hoh
            (piso bajo)
   upper...................PEE-soh AHL-toh
            (piso alto)
maid.......................kah-mah-RAY-rah
            (camarera)
room service...............sehr-BEE-see-oh
            (servicio)
```

I am sick.
Yoh ehs-TOY ehn-FEHR-moh.
(Yo estoy enfermo.)

Here is hoping you never have to be faced
with the words in this chapter. However, if
you do have a problem, these key phrases
and vocabulary words should help your unpleasant situation. Be sure to check chapter three, AT THE BORDER, pages 29 and 30,
for details regarding critical emergency
service.

Telling the Doctor Your Problem

My____hurts me............May DWAY-lay____.
        (Me duele____.)
I hurt my____.........May lahs-tee-MAY____.
        (Me lastimé____.)
My____is swollen..........Say een-CHOH____.
        (Se hinchó____.)
I am ill.........Ehs-TOY ehn-FEHR-moh (-a).
        (Estoy enfermo -a.)
My____is broken..........Say kay-BROH____.
        (Se quebró____.)
I cannot____..............Noh PWAY-doh____.
        (No puedo____.)
   breathe....................rehs-pee-RAHR
        (respirar)
   defecate................ehn-soo-see-AHR
        (ensuciar)
   urinate......................oh-ree-NAHR
        (orinar)
   walk.......................kah-mee-NAHR
        (caminar)

I have____....................TEHN-goh____.
        (Tengo____.)
   amoebic dysentery
    ..dees-ehn-tehr-EE-ah ah-may-bee-AH-nah
        (disentería amebiana)
   a backache.....doh-LOHR day ehs-PAHL-dah
        (dolor de espalda)
   a bruise.........OO-nah kohn-too-see-OHN
        (una contusión)
   a burn...................kay-mah-DOO-rah
        (quemadura)
   cramps...............lohs kah-LAHM-brays
        (los calambres)
   a cold..............oon rays-free-AH-doh
        (un resfriado)
    or......................kah-TAH-rroh
        (catarro)
   a cough........................oon tohs
        (un tos)

```
a cut.................OO-nah ay-REE-dah
            (una herida)
diarrhea................dee-ah-RRAY-ah
            (diarrea)
a fever............lah kah-lehn-TOO-rah
            (la calentura)
    or..................ehl fee-AY-bray
            (el fiebre)
the flu...................lah GREE-pah
            (la gripa)
a headache......doh-LOHR day kah-BAY-sah
            (dolor de cabeza)
indigestion.........een-dee-hehs-tee-OHN
            (indigestión, f)
a stomach ache
    .....oon doh-LOHR day ehs-TOH-mah-goh
        (un dolor de estómago)
a sunburn
    .....OO-nah kay-mah-DOO-rah day sohl
        (una quemadura de sol)

I have____.................See-EHN-toh____.
            (Siento____.)
chills..............ehs-kah-lah-FREE-ohs
            (esclalafríos)
pain........................doh-LOHR
            (dolor, m)

Where is____?........¿DOHN-day ehs-TAH____?
    (¿Dónde está____?)

I need____............Nay-say-SEE-toh____.
            (Necesito____.)

Take this three times a day in water.
  TOH-may EHS-toh trehs BAY-sehs ahl DEE-ah
            ehn AH-gwah.
  (Tome esto tres veces al día en agua.)

You must stay in bed.
  Oos-TEHD DAY-bay gwahr-DAHR ehn KAH-mah.
        (Ud. debe guardar en cama.)
```

145

```
Breathe......................Rehs-PEE-ray.
              (Respire.)
Exhale.......................Ehks-AH-lay.
              (Exhale.)
Inhale.......................Ahs-PEE-ray.
              (Aspire.)


ambulance..............ahm-boo-LAHN-see-ah
              (ambulancia)
clinic......................KLEE-nee-kah
              (clínica)
dentist.....................dehn-TEES-tah
              (dentista)
doctor..........................dohk-TOHR
              (doctor, m)
hospital....................ohs-pee-TAHL
              (hospital, m)
injection.................een-yehk-see-OHN
              (inyección)
medicine..................may-dee-SEE-nah
              (medicina)
nurse.......................ehn-FEHR-mah
              (enferma)
optometrist...............ohp-TOH-meh-trah
              (optómetra, m)
pharmacy..................fahr-MAH-see-ah
              (famacia)
   or.........................boh-TEE-kah
              (botica)
veterinarian.........beh-tay-ree-NAH-ree-oh
              (veterinario)
x-ray....................RAH-yohs EH-kees
              (rayos-X)
```

Items for the Medicine Chest

```
adhesive tape.........ehs-pah-rah-DRAH-poh
              (esparadrapo)
aspirin....................ahs-pee-REE-nah
              (aspirina)
```

bandage........................behn-DAH-hay
             (vendaje, m)
   or...........................BEHN-dah
             (venda, f)
boric acid..........AH-see-doh BOH-ree-koh
             (ácido bórico)
bromine........................BROH-moh
             (bromo)
calamine.................kah-lah-MEE-nah
             (calamina)
cough drop....pahs-TEE-yah PAH-rah lah tohs
          (pastilla para la tos)
cough syrup....hah-RAH-bay PAH-rah lah tohs
             (jarabe para la tos)
drops..........................GOH-tahs
             (gotas)
iodine.........................YOH-doh
             (yodo)
laxative....................lahks-AHN-tay
             (laxante, m)
   or.......................poor-GAHN-tay
             (purgante)
pill........................tah-BLAY-tah
             (tableta)
prescription...................ray-SAY-tah
             (receta)
quinine......................kee-NEE-nah
             (quinina)
talcum.........................TAHL-koh
             (talco)
thermometer..............tehr-MOH-may-troh
             (termómetro)

Parts of the Body

abdomen.......................ahb-DOH-mehn
             (abdomen, m)
ankle.........................toh-BEE-yoh
             (tobillo)
appendix...................ah-PEHN-dee-say
             (apéndice, m)

```
arm.............................BRAH-soh
              (brazo)
artery......................ahr-TEHR-ee‸ah
              (arteria)
back..........................ehs-PAHL-dah
              (espalda)
backbone, spine.......ehs-PEEN-ah dohr-SAHL
           (espina dorsal)
blood..........................SAHN-gray
              (sangre, f)
bone..............................WAY-soh
              (hueso)
bowels..................een-tehs-TEE-nohs
              (intestinos)
cheek.........................may-HEE-yah
              (mejilla)
chest...........................PAY-choh
              (pecho)
chin..........................bahr-BEE-yah
              (barbilla)
collar bone..............klah-BEE-koo-lah
             (clavícula)
ear...............................oh‸EE-doh
              (oído)
elbow.............................KOH-doh
              (codo)
eye...............................OH-hoh
              (ojo)
face.............................KAH-rah
              (cara)
finger...........................DAY-doh
              (dedo)
foot..............................pee‸AY
              (pie, m)
gall bladder...............bay-SEE-koo-lah
             (vesícula)
gland........................GLAHN-doo-lah
             (glándula)
hand.............................MAH-noh
              (mano, f)
head..........................kah-BAY-sah
              (cabeza)
```

```
heart........................koh-rah-SOHN
             (corazón, m)
heel..........................tah-LOHN
             (talón, m)
hip..........................kah-DAY-rah
             (cadera)
intestines...............een-tehs-TEE-nohs
             (intestinos)
jaw.......................mahn-DEE-boo-lah
             (mandíbula)
joint.............ahr-tee-koo-lah-see‿OHN
          (articulación, f)
kidney.........................ree-NYOHN
             (riñón)
leg..........................pee‿EHR-nah
             (pierna)
lip..........................LAH-bee‿oh
             (labio)
liver.........................EE-gah-doh
             (hígado)
lung.........................pool-MOHN
             (pulmón, m)
mouth........................BOH-kah
             (boca)
muscle.....................MOOS-koo-loh
             (músculo)
neck.........................KWAY-yoh
             (cuello)
nerve.......................NEHR-bee‿oh
             (nervio)
nose.........................nah-REES
             (nariz, f)
rectum......................REHK-toh
             (recto)
rib.........................kohs-TEE-yah
             (costilla)
shoulder.....................OHM-broh
             (hombro)
skin.........................pee‿EHL
             (piel, f)
spleen.......................BAH-soh
             (bazo)
```

149

```
stomach......................ehs-TOH-mah-goh
            (estómago)
tendon...........................tehn-DOHN
            (tendón, m)
thigh............................MOOS-loh
            (muslo)
throat.......................gahr-GAHN-tah
            (garganta)
thumb..........................pool-GAHR
            (pulgar)
toe....................DAY-doh day pee-AY
            (dedo de pie)
tongue.........................LEHN-gwah
            (lengua)
tonsils......................ahn-HEE-nahs
            (anginas)
vagina........................bah-HEEN-ah
            (vagina)
vein.............................BAY-nah
            (vena)
wrist........................moo-NYAY-kah
            (muñeca)
```

150

At the Dentist

The filling fell out.
.........Lah ehm-pahs-tah-DOO-rah say ah
        kah‑EE-doh.
   (La empastadura se ha caido.)

I need a____filling.
................Nay-say-SEE-toh OO-nah
          ehm-pahs-tah-DOO-rah day____.
   (Nesecito una empastadura de____.)

   gold.............................OH-roh
                   (oro)
   silver........................PLAH-tah
                   (plata)
   temporary.................tehm-poh-RAHL
                  (temporal)
   permanent.............pehr-mah-NEHN-tay
                  (permanente)
Do not extract it.........Noh loh SAH-kay.
          (No lo saque.)

Take out____...................SAH-kay____.
                (Saque____.)
   the molar...................lah MWAY-lah
                  (la muela)
   the tooth................oon dee‑EHN-tay
                  (un diente)
   the eyetooth............ehl kohl-MEE-yoh
                  (el colmillo)

I hurt here!..........¡May DWAY-lay ah-KAH!
            (¡Me duele acá!)
Novocain.................noh-boh-kah‑EE-nah
                  (novocaína)

If you have ever been fishing in the waters
off Baja or Mexico, you are acquainted with
some of the finest saltwater sport and game
fishing anywhere. If you have not tried
your hand with rod and reel in these blue
water deeps, you are in for a most pleasant
treat.

A fishing license is required for each non-resident alien, 14 years or older. This license covers both fresh and saltwater and is non-transferable. At this time, fees are in the process of being changed. When you buy your fishing license, you will be informed of the current rate.

There are bag limits and restrictions on certain species, on the type of equipment used and how fish must be dressed to take across the border. You will be informed about these restrictions when you receive the permit.

Mexican law states that shellfish can be purchased only at designated public markets. However, it is a very common practice along the deserted shores of Baja for native fishermen to come out to your boat and offer to trade abalone or lobster for 22 caliber shells, cigarettes, or whiskey. Although this practice is definitely frowned upon, I know few who can resist the inviting temptation of these freshly caught prizes.

Fishing licenses are obtained at sport fishing stores, tackle stores and some fuel docks in border towns, the American Automobile Association or from Mexican border officials. Once completed, the U.S. store will send them in to the proper authorities or you can mail them to:

The Mexican Government Fish Commission
395 West 6th Street
Room 3
San Pedro, CA 90731

FISH

```
abalone.........................ah-boo-LOHN
              (abulón, m)
albacore.....................ahl-bah-KOH-rah
              (albacora)
anchovy........................ahn-CHOH-ah
              (anchoa)
barnacle.......................pehr-SAY-bay
              (percebe, m)
barracuda..................bah-rrah-KOO-dah
              (barracuda)
bass...........................loh-BEE-nah
              (lobina)
   or..........................kah-BREE-yah
              (cabrilla)
black bass...........................MAY-roh
              (mero)
carp.................................KAHR-pah
              (carpa)
clam.............................ahl-MAY-hah
              (almeja)
cod..........................bah-kah-LAH-oh
              (bacalao)
crab...........................kahn-GRAY-hoh
              (cangrejo)
   the eating kind....................HI-bah
              (jaiba)
dolphin.........................dehl-FEEN
              (delfín, f)
   or..........................doh-LEE-nah
              (dolina)
dolphinfish....................doh-RAH-doh
              (dorado)
eel...........................ahn-GHEE-lah
              (anguila)
fillet.........................fee-LAY-tay
              (filete, m)
fish.................................pehs
              (pez, m)
   when it is cooked...........pehs-KAH-doh
              (pescado)
```

154

```
flounder......................lehn-GWAH-doh
              (lenguado)
garfish.......................pehs ah-GOO-hah
              (pez aguja)
grouper.......................gah-RROH-pah
              (garropa)
    or........................kah-BREE-yah
              (cabrilla)
hake..........................mehr-LOO-sah
              (merluza)
halibut.......................ah-lee-BOOT
              (halibut, f)
herring.......................ah-REHN-kay
              (arenque, f)
jellyfish.....................may-DOO-sah
              (medusa)
    or........................AH-gwah-MAH-lah
              (aguamala)
limpet........................LAH-pah
              (lapa)
lobster.......................lahn-GOHS-tah
              (langosta)
mackerel......................kah-BAH-yah
              (caballa)
    or........................ehs-KOHM-broh
              (escombro)
marlin........................MAHR-leen
              (marlin, m)
mullet........................LEE-sah
              (lisa)
octopus.......................POOL-poh
              (pulpo)
oyster........................OHS-trah
              (ostra)
    or........................ohs-tee-OHN
              (ostión, m)
perch.........................PEHR-kah
              (perca)
periwinkle....................lee-toh-REE-nah
              (litorina)
pompano.......................pah-loh-MAY-tah
              (palometa)
```

```
porpoise.....................toh-NEE-nah
               (tonina)
prawn....................lahn-gohs-TEEN
               (langostín)
ray.............................MAHN-tah
               (manta)
red snapper........PAHR-goh koh-loh-RAH-doh
            (pargo colorado)
    or..................whah-chee-NAHN-goh
               (huachinango)
roosterfish..................pehs GAH-yoh
               (pez gallo)
rudderfish.......................CHOH-pah
               (chopa, m)
sailfish...............ah-GOO-hah day mahr
               (aguja de mar)
    or.......................pehs BAY-lah
               (pez vela)
salmon.........................sahl-MOHN
               (salmón, f)
sand dollar...ehs-PAY-see-ay day ay-REE-soh
            (especie de erizo)
scallop..........moh-LOOS-koh bee-BAHL-boh
            (molusco bivalvo)
    or.........................bay-NAY-rah
               (venera)
sea bass.......................ROH-bah-loh
               (róbalo)
sea urchin.............ay-REE-soh day mahr
            (erizo de mar)
shark........................tee-boo-ROHN
               (tiburón, m)
shellfish....................mah-REES-koh
               (marisco)
shrimp.......................kah-mah-ROHN
               (camarón, m)
               (not camarero!)
sierra mackerel................see-AY-rrah
               (sierra)
skipjack.....................boh-NEE-toh
               (bonito)
```

```
snails (the eating kind)...kah-rah-KOH-lays
                (caracoles)
squid......................kah-lah-MAHR
                (calamar, m)
starfish.................ehs-tray-yah-MAHR
            (estrellamar, f)
stingray.................pahs-tee-NAH-kah
                (pastinaca)
swordfish................pehs ehs-PAH-dah
                (pez espada)
triggerfish..............pehs KOH-chee
                (pez cochi)
trout......................TROO-chah
                (trucha)
tuna.......................ah-TOON
                (atún, f)
whale......................bah-YAY-nah
                (ballena)
whitefish................koh-RAY-goh-noh
                (corégono)
yellowtail.................hoo-RAIL
                (jurel, m)
```

OTHER CREATURES

```
sea lion...................lay-OHN day mahr
                (león de mar)
sea snake........sehr-pee-EHN-tay day mahr
            (serpiente de mar)
turtle......................tohr-TOO-gah
                (tortuga)
whale.......................bah-YAY-nah
                (ballena)
```

BIRDS

```
dove........................pah-LOH-mah
                (paloma)
pelican....................pay-LEE-kah-noh
                (pelícano)
seagull....................gah-bee-OH-tah
                (gaviota)
```

CRITTERS

```
ant.........................ohr-MEE-gah
                (hormiga)
cockroach.................koo-kah-RAH-chah
                (cucaracha)
fly.........................MOHS-kah
                (mosca)
mosquito....................mohs-KEE-toh
                (mosquito)
mouse.......................rah-TOHN
                (ratón)
rat.........................RAH-tah
                (rata)
```

FISHING TERMS

Bad hook up.......Mahl ahn-sway-lee-AH-doh.
             (Mal anzueliado.)
bait.........................kahr-NAH-dah
             (carnada)
bait tank.....TAHN-kay PAH-rah kahr-NAH-dah
         (tanque para carnada)
Birds working.
         ....PAH-hah-rohs trah-bah-HAHN-doh.
             (Pájaros trabajando.)
to catch a fish..................pehs-KAHR
             (pescar)
Coming up.....................Ehl SOO-bay.
             (El sube.)
fish chair............SEE-yah day PEHS-kah
           (silla de pesca)
   hook.....................ahn-SWAY-loh
             (anzuelo)
   line.......................LEE-nay-ah
             (línca)
      or..........................say-DAHL
             (sedal, f)
market..............pehs-kah-dehr-EE-ah
             (pescadería)
net..................rehd day pehs-KAHR
             (red de pescar)
plug.......................ahn-SWAY-loh
             (anzuelo)
      or......................say-NUAY-loh
             (señuelo)
reel................................reel
    (that is right, it is the same!)
      or.................day-bahn-DAY-rah
             (devandera)
rod..........................KAH-nyah
             (caña)
ship..............BAHR-kah day PEHS-kah
           (barca de pesca)
spear........................ahr-POHN
             (arpón, m)

spoon hook.ahn-SWAY-loh day koo-CHAH-rah
(anzuelo de cuchara)

tackle..........ah-BEE⌢ohs day pehs-KAHR
(avíos de pescar)

fisherman....................pehs-kah-DOHR
(pescador, m)

Fish following........Lah pehs bee⌢EH-nay.
(La pez viene.)

fishing......................pehs-KAY-roh
(pesquero)

grounds....................pehs-KAY-rah
(pesquera)

or....................pehs-kayr-EE⌢ah
(pesquería)

gaff............................GAHN-choh
(gancho)

or........................GAHR-fee⌢oh
(garfio)

gill............................ah-GAH-yah
(agalla)

a jump...........................SAHL-toh
(salto)

kelp.........AHL-gah mah-REE-nah GRAHN-day
(alga marina grande)

leader........................ehm-PAH-tay
(empate, m)

scales........................ehs-KAH-mahs
(escamas)

to scale...................ehs-kah-MAHR
(escamar)

slack............................FLOH-hah
(floja)

Strike!..............¡Ehs-TAH hah-LAHN-doh!
(¡Está jalando!)

swivel..................dehs-tohr-say-DOHR
(destorcedor, m)

tangled....................ehn-ray-DAH-doh
(enredado)

to troll.......................troh-lay⌢AHR
(trolear)

160

My tire has a puncture.
Lah YAHN-tah tee-AY-nay oon ah-goo-HAY-roh.
(La llanta tiene un agujero.)

Driving in a foreign country is not for the
weak of heart--especially in places such as
Mexico City. La Reforma, the main street,
is a mind-boggling maze of traffic, blast-
ing horns and confusion. (As a pedestrian
trying to cross this street, it's even more
terrifying.)

Driving requires defensive tactics.

Roads and even major highways usually are not in as good a condition as those in the States and you're never quite sure what's around the corner or over the hill. It can be anything from a large truck driving down the middle line, a herd of cattle, a flock of sheep or road construction.

Roads are frequently narrow. I find myself reflexively breathing in, as if I could decrease the width of the vehicle by inhaling extra air, when sharing a skinny bridge with another vehicle.

In Puerto Rico, hand signals, not automatic turn signals, prevail. The native driver sticks his hand out the window and waves it in sort of a flapping, circular motion. This means anything from: I am stopping, turning left, right, pass me or slow down. Remember, stop signs say 'Pare,' not 'Alto,' in this country.

Street signs, if existing, can be hard to find or read. In Sevilla, Spain, for example, the names are on beautiful tiles, set about 10 feet from street level on the corners of buildings. Although attractive, they're impossible to read while battling traffic. Susie and I got so frustrated, we stopped, hired a cab, and followed him to the store location.

Have you ever been to Topolobampo, Mexico? Well, neither have I. This side trip taught me one other traveling tip: maps are not always accurate. I could clearly see this small village on the map (as could every other person I asked for directions), but trying to get there ended up as a comedy of errors.

The fellow car driver I asked for directions said: "Follow me." He, too, seemed surprised when the road we took dead-ended. The farmer said: "What do you want to go there for? There's nothing but mosquitos and swamp land." The Mexican Federale scratched his head and said: "I don't know, I've never been there." At this point, four hours later, I gave up.

One other word of caution: Do not drive at night unless absolutely necessary.

AUTOMOBILES, RV'S AND TRAILERS IN MEXICO

In addition to the Tourist Card, you must have a temporary importation permit for the car. These permits are usually issued at border entry points and are valid for the same period of time as tourist permits. To avoid being fined, you must remove your vehicle from Mexico before the permit expires. A car permit is not required in Baja but a motorist should carry proof of vehicle ownership. If you are in Baja and wish to go to the mainland by ferry, car permits are issued at ferry ports.

To get a car permit, you must have proof of U.S. citizenship, a valid U.S. driver's license, the vehicle registration or a notarized bill of sale for the vehicle, trailer or motorcycle. If the vehicle is registered in a company name, a notarized letter from the company authorizing the use of the vehicle in Mexico is required. Permits are free.

INSURANCE

The purchase of Mexican car insurance is not mandatory in all states; however, it is highly recommended. It's available in most cities and towns on the U.S. side of the border and should be purchased prior to entering Mexico. U.S. automobile liability insurance is not valid in Mexico. If you are involved in an accident, you cannot establish proof of your ability to pay unless you have a valid Mexican policy. Drivers may be detained until liability has been established and run the risk of spending time in jail, even if the case is eventually decided in their favor.

If you are involved in an accident or receive a citation, your driver's license will be held until you have paid the fine. Because Mexican police officers aren't permitted to hold a driver's license that has been issued by another country, they will ask you to follow them to the nearest police station. There you pay the fine and receive an official receipt. You shouldn't consider yourself under arrest while following the above procedure. It has been instituted so that non-Mexicans won't have to return to the country just to keep a court date and, perhaps, pay a fine.

You may not sell, transfer, or otherwise dispose of a car brought into Mexico under the temporary importation permit, nor leave Mexico without the car. In case of emergencies or accidents where the car becomes inoperable or unrepairable, arrangements to depart Mexico without the car can be made by the owner through the Mexican Federal Registry of Automobiles in Mexico City or through the local offices of the Treasury

Department (Hacienda). The U.S. Embassy or Consulates can assist in such cases.

The owner of the car should not allow anyone else to drive it unless he is in the vehicle. To do so can result in confiscation of the car and/or a heavy fine.

FUEL

Gasoline is readily available in all of Mexico. The government-owned Pemex stations are found in virtually all cities and towns. Two grades of gas are sold: Extra, their premium, is unleaded, has an octane rating of 92 and is in the silver pumps. Nova, regular, contains lead, has an 81-octane rating and is in the blue pumps. 1975 and newer U.S. cars cannot use Nova. Diesel fuel is found in the red pumps.

Trucks and cars are notorious for not running well on Mexican gas, especially those that need high-octane, leaded fuel. If pinging or loss of power occurs, use an additive in your tank.

Mexican gasoline may contain water or other undesirable goodies. To prevent clogged fuel line and carburetor jets, be ready to clean or replace in-line fuel filters. Many travelers strain the fuel through a chamois to prevent impurities from entering the tank.

You should be prepared to check your own water, oil, air in the tires, and wash your windows. You might want to carry a supply of cloths or toweling for this purpose as, generally, they are not available. If the attendant does it for you, a tip is usually in order.

Don't count on the next little town having fuel. Even if your tank is half full--or half empty--fill up before you leave. Although stations are plentiful, that does not always mean they're open for business.

SPARES

Rest assured, if something is going to break, it will--when you're far from a town and in the middle of nowhere. Naturally, you cannot take a full garage of tools with you, but do take those items that might help you successfully fix a minor break-down. Extra air filters, brake fluid, fuses, belts, hoses, power steering fluid, water for the radiator and flares are prac-tical additions to your vehicle. If you are traveling into truly remote areas, you might want to secure additional water and fuel tanks to your car or motor home.

If your engine or diesel, or major applian-ce should need parts or repairs, or if you need to locate a specific tool or repair-man, the words for these necessities are found in the chapter ENGINES AND TOOLS--Repairs and Servicing, pages 221-241.

GREEN ANGELS

The Angeles Verdes patrol the major north and south highways in mainland Mexico and Highway 1 and 5 in Baja with radio-control-led units to supply assistance and protec-tion for any motorist in distress. There is no charge for their time, but if the car problem is due to a part that must be replaced, you will, of course, have to bear that expense. If you have an accident or otherwise feel too ill to drive, the Green Angels will render first aid. In case of an emergency, they will communicate by radio for you. Green Angels also are equipped with CB's to receive your messages.

CB'S

Tourists are allowed to operate CB radios while in Mexico. A fee is required for the permit that can be obtained from a Mexican Consulate or an office of the Mexican National Tourism Council before leaving the States. Permits are not issued at the border.

According to the Mexican government, transmissions on CB equipment are allowed on Channel 9 (emergency only), 10 (intercommunication) and 11 (localization). They may be used only for personal communication and emergency road assistance. Any form of linear amplifier or other device that increases the transmission power to over 5 watts is prohibited. CB equipment may not be used near radio installations of the aeronautical or marine services.

TRAILERS

A trailer measuring more than 8-feet in width and 40-feet in length requires a special permit that is obtained at the Federal Highway Police Road Office. Permits are issued at the discretion of the offical since road conditions in much of Baja, for example, make trailer travel prohibitive and many back country roads and some paved highways are not wide enough to accommodate large trailers.

VOCABULARY

```
I need____.............Nay-say-SEE-toh____.
              (Necesito____.)
Do you have____?..¿Tee-AY-nay oos-TEHD____?
              (¿Tiene ud.____?)
Where is____?........¿DOHN-day ehs-TAH____?
              (¿Dónde está____?)
```

```
The____does not work.
..............Noh foonk-see-OH-nah____.
              (No funciona____.)
```

```
The____is leaking.
...........Ehs-TAH goh-tay-AHN-doh____.
              (Está goteando____.)
```

```
Where can I dump my holding tank?
    ¿DOHN-day ehs-TAH oon loo-GAHR PAH-rah
    boh-TAHR ehl AH-gwah ehs-koo-SAH-doh?
      (¿Dónde está un lugar para botar
              el agua escusado?)
```

```
My tire has a puncture.
Lah YAHN-tah tee-AY-nay oon ah-goo-HAY-roh.
      (La llanta tiene un agujero.)
```

```
The tire is flat.
    Lah YAHN-tah ehs-TAH day-seen-FLAH-dah.
      (La llanta está desinflada.)
```

```
Do you want to help me change the tire?
..........¿Kee-AY-ray ah-yoo-DAHR-may ah
    kahm-bee-AHR lah YAHN-tah?
  (¿Quiere ayudarme a cambiar la llanta?)
```

```
My car has broken down.
......Say may ah days-kohm-PWAYS-toh ehl
              KAH-rroh.
    (Se me ha descompuesto el carro.)
```

168

Send someone to repair my car.
..MAHN-day ah ahl-gee^EHN ah ray-pah-RAHR
            mee KAH-rroh.
   (Mande a alguien a reparar mi carro.)

accelerator.............ah-say-lay-rah-DOHR
            (acelerador, m)
accessory....................ow-MEHN-toh
             (aumento)
air conditioning
   ......EYE-ray ah-kohn-dee-see^ohn-AH-doh
         (aire (m) acondicionado)
air pump.........................BOHM-bah
              (bomba)
axle................................AY-hay
             (eje, m)
   front.............AY-hay ah-day-LAHN-tay
            (eje adelante)
   rear................AY-hay trah-SAY-roh
            (eje trasero)
   shaft.......................PWEHN-tay
              (puente, m)
bath tub..........................TAY-nah
             (tena)
belt.....koh-RRAY-ah day trahns-mee-see^OHN
        (correa de transmisión)
body (auto).............kah-rroh-sehr-EE^ah
             (carrocería)
brake.............................FRAY-noh
              (freno)
   drum.............tahm-BOHR day FRAY-noh
           (tambor de freno)
   hand...............FRAY-noh day MAH-noh
            (freno de mano)
   lining.............FOH-rroh day FRAY-noh
            (forro de freno)
   shoe...........sah-PAH-tah day FRAY-noh
            (zapata de freno)
bumper...................pah-rah-CHOH-kays
            (parachoques, f)
   or.......................day-FEHN-sah
              (defensa)

169

```
butane........................boo-TAH-noh
                (butano)
car...........................KAH-rroh
                (carro)
   or.........................KOH-chay
                (coche, m)
car title..TEE-too-loh day proh-pee-ay-DAHD
        (título de propiedad)
   registration.......ray-hees-trah-see-OHN
                (registraoión)
chassis.......................CHAH-sees
                (chasis, m)
   motor number....NOO-may-roh day moh-TOHR
                (número de motor)
collision.....................CHOH-kay
                (choque, m)
dashboard.....................tah-BLAY-roh
                (tablero)
diesel........................DEE-sehl
                (diesel, m)
door..........................pohr-tay-SWAY-lah
                (portezuela)
drive shaft...................kahr-DAHN
                (cardán, m)
drivers license
      .......lee-SEHN-see-ah day mah-nay-HAHR
            (licencia de manejar)
fender........................ah-LAY-roh
                (alero)
   or.........................gwahr-dah-LOH-dohs
                (guardalodos)
flashlight....................LAHM-pah-rah
                (lámpara)
flat..........................day-seen-FLAH-dah
                (desinflada)
   or.........................peen-CHAH-soh
                (pinchazo)
fluid.........................FLOO-ee-doh
                (flúido)
   brake.........FLOO-ee-doh day FRAY-noh
            (flúido de freno)
```

garage.........................gah-RAH-hay
                (garaje, m)
   or..tah-YEHR day ray-pah-rah-see⌣OHN-ays
          (taller de reparaciones)
gas..........................gah-soh-LEE-nah
                (gasolina)
   cap...........................tah-POHN
                (tapón, m)
   line..too-bay-REE⌣ah day gah-soh-LEE-nah
          (tubería de gasolina)
   station
        ehs-tah-see⌣OHN day gah-soh-LEE-nah
          (estación de gasolina)
   tank...................gah-SOH-may-tehr
               (gasómeter, m)
glove compartment..........kah-whay-LEE-tah
                (cajuelita)
Green Angels.........AHN-hay-lays BEHR-days
            (Angeles Verdes)
headlamp bulb.........FOH-koh dehl fah-ROHL
                (foco del farol)
headlight..........................FAH-roh
                  (faro)
heater..................kah-lehn-tah-DOHR
             (calentador, m)
holding tank
   TAHN-kay PAH-rah AH-gwah ehs-koo-SAH-doh
     (tanque (f) para agua escusado)
hood...............................KOH-fray
                (cofre, m)
hook-ups......................ehn-foo-CHAHR
                (enfuchar)
horn...........................KLAH-ksohn
                (klaxon, m)
   or...........................boh-SEE-nah
                (bocina)
hub cap....................tah-pah-DAY-rah
                (tapadera)
ice................................YAY-loh
                 (heilo)
ice box.......................nay-BAY-rah
                (nevera)

or..........................yay-LAY-roh
                 (hielero)
jack..............................GAH-toh
                 (gato)
key...............................YAH-bay
                 (llave, f)
leak..........................goh-TAY-rah
                 (gotera)
license plate.....................PLAH-kah
                 (placa)
lights............................FAH-rohs
                 (faros)
to lubricate.................loo-bree-KAHR
                 (lubricar)
make (Ford, Datsun)...............MAHR-koh
                 (marco)
map...............................MAH-pah
                 (mapa, m)
number of____..........NOO-may-roh day____
              (número de____)
   doors........................PWEHR-tahs
                 (puertas)
   cylinders................see-LEEN-drohs
                 (cilindros)
   passengers.............pah-sah-HAY-rohs
                 (pasajeros)
parts for a car........ray-fah-ksee^OHN-ays
                 (refacciones, m)
   to park..............ehs-tah-see^ohn-AHR
                 (estacionar)
propane.......................proh-PAH-noh
                 (propano)
puncture...................ah-goo^HAY-roh
                 (agujero)
to push.......................ehm-poo-HAHR
                 (empujar)
radio..........................RAH-dee^oh
                 (radio)
radio tube...........TOO-boh day RAH-dee^oh
              (tubo de radio)
refrigerator..........ray-free-hay-rah-DOHR
                 (refrigerador, m)

172

road map......MAH-pah day kah-rray-TAY-rahs
        (mapa (m) de carreteras)
shock absorber........ah-mohr-tee-gwah-DOHR
            (amortiguador, m)
shower...........................DOO-chah
            (ducha)
speedometer............bay-loh-SEE-may-troh
            (velocímetro, m)
steering column
    ......koh-LOOM-nah day dee-rayk-see-OHN
        (columna de dirección)
steering wheel................boh-LAHN-tay
            (volante, m)
stove.........................ehs-TOO-fah
            (estufa)
tail light............fah-ROHL trah-SAY-roh
            (farol (m) trasero)
tank.............................TAHN-kay
            (tanque, m)
tire............................YAHN-tah
            (llanta)
tow truck.....................ray-MOHL-kay
            (remolque, m)
    rope.........................SOH-gah
            (soga)
    to tow...................ray-mohl-KAHR
            (remolcar)
truck.........................kah-mee-OHN
            (camión, m)
    pickup.......................peek-AHP
            (pickap, m)
trunk........................kah-WHAY-lah
            (cajuela)
tube........................KAH-mah-rah
            (cámara)
universal joint.kroo-SAY-tah dehl kahr-DAHN
            (cruzeta del cardán)
to wash........................lah-BAHR
            (lavar)
water...........................AH-gwah
            (agua, m)

water heater..kah-lehn-tah-DOHR day AH-gwah
       (calentador de agua)
window......................behn-TAH-nah
       (ventana)
  or.........................BEE-dree‿oh
       (vidrio)
windshield...............pah-rah-BREE-sah
       (parabrisa)
windshield wiper
  ...leem-pee‿ah-DOHR day pah-rah-BREE-sah
      (limpiador de parabrisa)
a witness....................tehs-TEE-goh
       (testigo)
year of car..................moh-DAY-loh
       (modelo)
  or............................AH-nyoh
       (año)

ON THE HIGHWAY

How far is____?
  ...¿Ah kay dees-TAHN-see‿ah ehs-TAH____?
    (¿A qué distancia está____?)

Is this the way to____?
  ....¿Ehs EHS-tay ehl kah-MEE-noh kay bah
         ah____?
    (¿Es éste el camino que va a____?)

Which is the road to____?
  .¿Kwahl ehs lah kah-rray-TAY-rah ah____?
    (¿Cuál es la carretera a____?)

Are the roads to____good?
  ..¿Sohn BWAY-nahs lahs kah-rray-TAY-rahs
             ah____?
    (¿Son buenas las carreteras a____?)

Can you draw me a map of the way?
  .....¿PWAY-day oos-TEHD dee-boo-HAHR-may
      oon MAH-pah dehl kah-MEE-noh?
  (Puede ud. dibujarme un mapa del camino?)

174

Please direct me to____.
..Pohr fah-BOHR, dee-REE-hah-may ah____.
        (Por favor, diríjame a____.)

Where can I find____?
........¿DOHN-day PWAY-doh ah-YAHR____?
        (¿Dónde puedo hallar____?)
May I park here?
  ¿PWAY-doh ehs-tah-see⌢ohn-AHR-may ah-KEE?
        (¿Puedo estacionarme aquí?)

Where is____?........¿DOHN-day ehs-TAH____?
        (¿Dónde está____?)

It is (not) far.....(Noh) Ehs-TAH LAY-hohs.
        (No) está lejos.)

Follow this road.
    ..SEE-gah lah MEES-mah kah-rray-TAY-rah.
        (Siga la misma carretera.)

Turn right (left) at the next____.
  TOH-may soo day-RAY-chah (ees-kee⌢EHR-dah)
        ehn lah PROH-ksee-mah____.
        (Tome su derecha (izquierda) en la
                próxima____.)

avenue....................ah-bay-NEE-dah
                (avenida)
boulevard...................boo-lay-BAHR
                (bulevar, m)
bridge..........................PWEHN-tay
                (puente, m or f)
crossroad.............ehn-kroo-see-HAH-dah
                (encrucijada)
dirt road.................day tee⌢AY-rrah
                (de tierra)
  on road maps, sometimes spelled
  ....tah-rrah-SEHR-ee⌢ah
                (tarraceria)
highway..................kah-rray-TAY-rah
                (carretera)

175

```
federal....................fay-deh-RAHL
            (federal)
state......................ehs-TAH-doh
            (estado)
kilometer..............kee-LOH-may-troh
            (kilómetro)
left side..........LAH-doh ees-kee-EHR-doh
            (lado izquierdo)
narrow (road)...............ehs-TRAY-choh
            (estrecho)
paved road.............pah-bee-mehn-TAH-doh
            (pavimentado)
right side.............LAH-doh day-RAY-choh
            (lado derecho)
road.......................kah-MEE-noh
            (camino)
roadside inn...................poh-SAH-dah
            (posada)
street.........................KAH-yay
            (calle, f)
```

KILOMETERS (PER HOUR) TO MILES (PER HOUR)

Miles	Kilometers
.62	1
1.24	2
1.86	3
2.48	4
3.10	5
3.72	6
4.34	7
4.96	8
5.58	9
6.20	10
12.40	20
18.60	30
24.80	40
31.00	50
37.20	60
43.40	70
49.60	80
55.80	90
62.00	100
68.20	110
74.40	120
80.60	130
86.80	140
93.00	150

ROAD SIGNS

STOP

ESCUELA
School

PUENTE ANGOSTO
Narrow Bridge

CRUCE F.C.
Railroad Crossing

Yield Right of Way

GANADO
Cattle

HOMBRES TRABAJANDO
Men Working

VADO
Dip

ZONA DE DERRUMBES
Slide Area

CURVA PELIGROSA
Dangerous Curve

CAMINO SINUOSO
Winding Road

Speed Limit

Two Way

Left Turn Only

One Way

One Hour Parking

PROHIBIDO ESTACIONARSE
No Parking

No Parking
8 a.m. to 9 p.m.

NO VOLTEAR EN U
No U Turn

Keep to the Right

Slow   **Detour**   **Road Closed**

TRAILER PARK   **AIRPORT**   **FERRY**

RESTAURANT-BAR   **MEDICAL SERVICES**   **TELEPHONE**

GAS & MECHANICAL SERVICE

Bob and Jinny Ristau, private pilots with numerous air trips to Baja, chuckled over one word in the vocabulary section of this chapter.

"Hangars? You won't find them in Baja!" exclaims Jinny."

"Take along tie-downs and protection for the intakes on your engine because your aircraft will be outside."

"And," both agreed, "make sure your plane is thoroughly secured and you have all necessary personal gear <u>before</u> leaving the air field. Frequently, the closest town is a long distance--and ends up being an expensive ride if you must return for forgotten chores or items."

ENTERING MEXICO

In addition to the Tourist Card, Third Party Liability Insurance must be written by a Mexican insurance company to satisfy the Civil Responsibility Act for property damage or bodily injury caused to others. Your U.S. policy will probably cover the aircraft hull and passenger and crew liability. However, check with your insurance company before leaving. Leased, rented or borrowed aircraft, just like a vehicle, should have notarized permission, written on letterhead paper from the company or individual who owns the craft.

You must file a border-crossing flight plan with a U.S. FAA Flight Service Station at least 30 minutes prior to crossing the border into Mexico. A request for Mexican Customs and Immigration should be made at the same time. Prior to your first landing, close your U.S. Border Crossing Flight Plan by radio with the FAA.

All flight plans into Mexico must be opened and closed in writing and closed as soon as possible after landing. All tourist piston aircraft with less than 16 seats are required to make their first landing at an Airport of Entry closest to the border.

An aircraft with the necessary fuel capacity and range to reach Hermosillo or Guaymas can use these two airports as its first landing port. On your initial contact for clearance with Mexican authorities, inform them that you are flying directly to these ports. Check before you leave for other ports of entry if these are not the areas you wish to visit.

Upon landing, the pilot will be directed to a designated parking area. Everyone aboard should proceed to the Airport Operations Office, 'Comandancia,' where an arrival report, general declaration form and flight plan for the next section of the journey will be filed. The pilot needs to show his license, aircraft registration and airworthiness certificate, and proof of Mexican Liability Insurance at this time. Proceed to Immigration, Customs and return to the Comandancia.

A flight plan fee is charged for each segment of the journey. Previously, this fee was included in the fuel costs but because of accounting problems, the fee is now collected separately.

Several companies, for a fee, will fill out all the necessary forms for Mexican Insurance or any other specific licenses you may need. One such company is Mexair.

For further information, write to or phone:

Mexair Insurance Brokers
12601 Venice Boulevard
Los Angeles, CA 90066

phone: (213) 398-5797

FUEL

Federal airports have standard rates for gas and major credit cards such as Master-Card and Visa are accepted; however, occasionally the terminal is out of the specific charge slip so you should be prepared to pay cash, particularly in smaller air ports. Smaller airfields can charge any price they choose for fuel.

Major airports have 100 and 80 octane fuel. Because Mexican gas can contain impurities, the Ristaus suggest straining the fuel through a chamois.

"And be prepared to see your cans or barrels of fuel delivered to the plane in a wheelbarrow at smaller, dirt-strip runways!"

GENERAL INFORMATION

Jinny suggests taking insect repellent, sunglasses--and small change for tipping. "Additional water and survival equipment is an important consideration if you are going across the desolate areas of Baja," she states.

"Remember to ask others familiar with the areas about local information. Channel 122.9 is the plane-to-plane channel and 122.8, Unicom, for privately owned airports. Both channels are used to broadcast landing information at non-controlled airports."

"You should have no problems flying into Mexico," Bob says, "as long as you follow the rules. Unless you have an instrument rating, night flying is prohibited."

EXITING MEXICO

To exit Mexico before returning to the U.S., the last landing must be at one of the Mexican Ports of Entry. The original general declaration form, flight plan and tourist card is turned into the Out Processing Official. No further landing may be made in Mexico without clearing the country again. The same crew on board when the aircraft entered Mexico must be aboard when the aircraft departs unless a change has been approved by the Commandant. Next, file a U.S. Border Crossing flight plan with the Mexican Operation Office.

The first U.S. landing must be at an International Airport of Entry. Pilots should contact the FAA/FSS by radio before the final landing in Mexico to alert U.S. Customs of the stateside ETA and give them the necessary 30 minute advance notice. Include in this transmission the aircraft ID number, type, position, airport of departure, pilot name, number of people aboard and their citizenship. Failure to notify U.S. Customs prior to landing can result in a $500 fine.

The following vocabulary includes only airplane parts or words geared to flying. Two other chapters contain information valuable to aircraft: ENGINES AND TOOLS--Repairs and Servicing, pages 221-241 and NAVIGATION--Charts, Instruments and Weather, pages 242-252.

VOCABULARY

aileron......................eye-lay-ROHN
              (ailerón, m)
air..............................EYE-ray
              (aire, m)
air line..............LEE-nee⌢ah AIR-ay⌢ah
              (línea aérea)
air pocket.....................BAH-chay
              (bache, m)
airfoil...........................AH-lah
              (ala)
   or....PLAH-noh ah⌢ay-roh-dee-NAH-mee-koh
          (plano aerodinámico)
airman, aviator.............ah-bee⌢ah-DOHR
              (aviador, m)
   aviatrix...............ah-bee⌢ah-TREES
              (aviatriz, f)
airplane................ah⌢ay-roh-PLAH-noh
              (aeroplano)
   or.........................ah-bee⌢OHN
              (avión, m)
   private airplane.......ah-bee⌢oh-NAY-tah
              (avioneta)
airport................ah⌢ay-roh-PWEHR-toh
              (aeropuerto)
airsick.....................ah-tah-KAH-doh
              (atacado)
aloft.......................ah-RREE-bah
              (arriba)
   or.........................ehn AHL-toh
              (en alto)
altimeter.................ahl-TEE-may-troh
              (altímetro)
altitude....................ahl-tee-TOOD
              (altitud, f)
aviation................ah-bee⌢ah-see⌢OHN
              (aviación)
brake............................FRAY-noh
              (freno)
chart...........................KAHR-tah
              (carta)

```
ceiling..........................TAY-choh
                (techo)
cockpit.......................kah-BEE-nah
                (cabina)
commandant...............koh-mahn-DAHN-tay
                (comandante)
control cables.....KAH-blays day kohn-TROHL
            (cables de control)
   pedal..........................pay-DAHL
                (pedal, m)
   stick.........................bahs-TOHN
                (bastón, m)
   tower...........TOH-rray day kohn-TROHL
            (torre (m) de control)
controller (traffic).....kohn-troh-lah-DOHR
                (controlador, m)
co-pilot....................koh-pee-LOH-toh
                (copiloto)
course...........................ROOM-boh
                (rumbo)
DME (the same)........................DME
dispatcher..............dehs-pah-chah-DOHR
            (despachador, m)
down..........................ah-BAH-hoh
                (abajo)
flight plan.............plahn day BWAY-loh
            (plan de vuelo)
fuel, jet.................toor-boh-SEE-nah
                (turbosina)
fuselage..................foo-say-LAH-hay
                (fuselaje, m)
gasoline..................gah-soh-LEE-nah
                (gasolina)
gate...........................PWEHR-tah
                (puerta)
hangar..........................ahn-GAHR
                (hangar, m)
jet (the same)........................jet
to land...................ah-tay-rree-SAHR
                (aterrizar)
landing...............ah-tay-rree-SAH-hay
                (aterrizaje)
```

```
field...KAHM-poh day ah-tay-rree-SAH-hay
        (campo de aterrizaje)
gear.......trehn day ah-tay-rree-SAH-hay
        (tren (m) de aterrizaje)
strip...........................PEES-tah
                (pista)
wheels
  ...roo⌢AY-dahs day ah-tay-rree-SAH-hay
        (ruedas de atterrizaje)
legal papers......pah-PAY-lays lay-GAH-lays
            (papeles legales)
magneto.....................mahg-NAY-toh
              (magneto, f)
map.............................MAH-pah
                (mapa)
octane......................ohk-TAH-noh
              (octano)
  80 octane.......oh-CHEHN-tah ohk-TAH-noh
        (ochento octano)
  100 octane..........see⌢EHN ohk-TAH-noh
        (cien octano)
oil...........................ah-SAY-tay
              (aceite, m)
change the oil
    ..........KAHM-bee⌢oh day ah-SAY-tay
        (cambio de aceite)
  40 wt.............GRAH-doh oh-CHEHN-tah*
        (grado ochenta)
  50 wt.................GRAH-doh see⌢EHN*
        (grado cien)
Operations Office......koh-mahn-DAHN-see⌢ah
            (Comandancia)
parachute..............pah-rah-kah⌢EE-dahs
            (paracaídas)
passenger..................pah-sah-HAY-roh
              (pasajero)
pilot.........................pee-LOH-toh
              (piloto)
propeller.......................AY-lee-say
              (hélice, m)

*Saybolt scale

                    188
```

```
radio.........................RAH-dee-oh
              (radio, m)
registration.........ray-hees-trah-see-OHN
          (registración, f)
route.........................ROO-tah
              (ruta)
rudder.......................tee-MOHN
              (timón, m)
runway.......................PEES-tah
              (pista)
runway lights.....LOO-says day lah PEES-tah
          (luces (f) de la pista)
sea plane...............ee-droh-ah-bee-OHN
              (hidroavión, m)
seat.........................SEE-yah
              (silla)
stabilizer.........ehs-tah-bee-lee-sah-DOHR
          (estabilizador, m)
to stall....................ehs-tah-LAHR
              (estalar)
stops (fuel)..................ehs-KAH-lahs
              (escalas)
tail................PLAH-nohs day KOH-lah
          (planos de cola)
  or..........................KOH-lah
              (cola)
  fin.....PLAH-noh day day-REE-bah KOH-lah
          (plano de deriva cola)
  skid...............pah-TEEN day KOH-lah
              (patín de cola)
  spin......................bah-RRAY-nah
              (barrena)
    or.........................ehs-PEEN
              (espin, m)
  unit..........kohn-HOON-toh day KOH-lah
          (cojunto de cola)
  wind............bee-EHN-toh day KOH-lah
          (viento de cola)
  to tail spin
    ......dehs-sehn-DEHR ehn bah-RRAY-nah
          (descender en barrena)
```

```
tank............................TAHN-kay
              (tanque, m)
   right............TAHN-kay day-RAY-choh
           (tanque derecho)
   left...........TAHN-kay ees-kee^EHR-doh
           (tanque izquierdo)
   rear..........TAHN-kay pohs-tay-ree^OHR
           (tanque posterior)
   tip....................TAHN-kays teeps
              (tanques tips)
   wing..................TAHN-kays AH-lahs
              (tanques alas)
tire............................YAHN-tah
              (llanta)
up............................ah-RREE-bah
              (arriba)
VOR................................bohr
                (VOR)
wind.........................bee^EHN-toh
              (viento)
   direction......ROOM-boh dehl bee^EHN-toh
           (rumbo del viento)
windshield................pah-rah-BREE-sah
              (parabrisa)
windshield wiper
   ...leem-pee^ah-DOHR day pah-rah-BREE-sah
        (limpiador de parabrisa)
windsock......................choh-REE-soh
              (chorizo)
wing............................AH-lah
              (ala)
```

190

Man overboard!
¡OHM-bray ahl AH-gwah!
(¡Hombre al agua!)

Cruising the warm, clear waters of Mexico is a delightful experience. Swimming, snorkeling, diving, fishing--enjoying the waters to the fullest are a few of the offshoots of visiting Mexico by water...not to mention quiet, secluded anchorages with miles and miles of sandy beach.

Before you leave the States, you should have the boat's registration papers, a notarized affidavit of permission from the owner if you do not own the vessel, Tourist Cards (pages 22-23), personal fishing licenses (page 153), and a boat permit for recreational boating. This permit is sold for a calendar year by the Mexican Department of Fisheries.

In addition, you must fill out a Crew and Passenger List, 'Lista de Tripulante--Yate de Placer.' These forms are available at marine supply stores and chart centers. They are good for one month and can be renewed while in Mexico. Make several copies because you will need to hand them out to the various Port Captains along your route.

The document is written in Spanish and must be filled out, in triplicate, in Spanish. When completed, it should be taken to the Mexican Consul for official processing.

Although this form seems to be a simple one page document, if you are not familiar with the wording it looks like an unsolvable maze. Below is what goes in the blanks--and do not forget, where applicable, you must use the Spanish word.

"Del yate de placer estadounidense (name of vessel) del porte de (gross tonnage) toneladas brutas y (net tonnage) netas, con matricula número (registration number) del Puerto de (port of departure) declara que el día (day of departure) de (month) de 19__ (year), zarpara con destino al Puerto de (Mexican port destination) al mando del Capitan (name of Captain) con escala in los puertos (ports of call)."

Below this is a crew list with the following headings:

Nombre (name)
Nacionalidad (citizenship)
Edad (age)
Cargo a Bordo (title: captain, cook, etc.
    see page 200 and 201)

Improper completion of this form can cause
extensive delays. Therefore, yacht documentation companies are available that, for a
fee, will handle all the details for you.

One such firm is:
Mexican Yacht Documentation Service
12601 Venice Blvd.
Los Angeles, CA, 90066
phone: (213) 398-5797

According to Raul Martinez of this company,
they will process the papers, obtain fishing licenses and gun permits, write Mexican
Insurance or handle any other specific
needs. Martinez states, "People do not have
the necessary information 90% of the time
which causes delays in the processing of
the documents. Even if you do fill out your
own papers, take them to a broker for a
final check to make sure you have all the
necessary forms."

Temporary Import Permits are obtained AFTER
you arrive in Mexico and generally necessary only in Mainland Mexico, not Baja. Ask
the Port Captain how and where to obtain
the permit in the your area.

In some ports, Fuel Permits are required.
You will be told when these are necessary.

TRAILERABLE BOATS

Trailerable boats are permitted in Mexico and are considered as any other trailerable item. A small per month and per ton registration fee is payable at the time of departure. Boats more than 22 feet in length are required to place a bond that guarantees the customs duties they may cause. You will probably have to buy a fishing license (see page 153).

Buy Mexican boat insurance at the same time you purchase your vehicle insurance.

CHARTERING BOATS

Chartering, especially when it comes to sport fishing boats, is popular in Mexico. Almost any fishing port has boats for charter with a Mexican skipper who knows the nearby waters. Rates vary according to the length of the trip, the size of the vessel and the accommodations and services offered. Generally, the fishing license fee is included in the charter cost and is obtained by the native skipper.

Yacht chartering is rare although smaller boats can be rented by the day or week.

INSURANCE

Check with your insurance agent about your boat policy. Most Southern Californian issuing companies have coverage from Point Conception to Río Santa Tomas, approximately 20 miles south of Ensenada. To extend the policy for additional southern ports, a rider must be added.

Scott Jarvie, Overseas Insurance Co., San Diego, says, "This rider will increase your already existing premium and usually increases the deductible. Insurance companies will not write a policy from June 1 through October 1." This is the Chubasco or tropical storm season for Mexico.

A trip surveyor endorsement is frequently required by the insurance company in addition to a current boat survey. In this case, the surveyor looks at the seaworthiness of the vessel, inquires about the experience and health of the captain and crew, and makes sure ample spares and emergency equipment are aboard.

W. David Cookingham, surveyor, Maritime Service Co., San Diego, points out, "Some effort should be made to choose a surveyor with personal cruising experience in a vessel similiar to yours. Most of the Merchant Marine surveyors have unrealistic opinions regarding the small boat cruiser because of lack of sea time in small boats. If your intended cruise will take you to new ports of call, a surveyor can act as a cruise consultant. His first-hand experiences can be invaluable when it comes to navigation or local knowledge of an area."

In addition to the extended U.S. boat policy, Mexican insurance is a plus. In the event of an accident, just as in the case of autos, the Mexican policy, not the U.S. one, is recognized.

FIRST PORT OF ENTRY

When you arrive at your first Mexican Port of Entry, you must visit certain governmental offices to get clearance. Take ashore: the crew list, tourist cards and passports. The only person who is permitted to go ashore is the captain. Also, note that the captain is responsible for the actions of each crew member at all times.

There is no set rule as to whom you see first although the following procedure is generally the accepted one. 1) Find the Port Captain. 2) Proceed to Immigration. 3) Go to Customs. 4) Return to the Port Captain with all the papers properly processed. After clearance, all are free to go ashore.

You must go through this procedure any time you stop in a port and want to go ashore.

Time consuming? You better believe it! These offices rarely are close to each other and lunch hours or official business seems to make the necessary person unavailable. Be prepared to be gone from the vessel for quite a while. And a cold beer while you wait will never taste better.

FLAGS

A flag of the country you are visiting should be flown from the highest halyard or available place. The U.S. flag is displayed from the transom.

"WINTERIZING"

You have spent the last six months or more getting your boat ready for this voyage. Everything is running properly as you cruise to Cabo or Guaymas or wherever, to anchor, bask in the sun and enjoy your leisure. What you may not have taken into account is that you are, or will be, letting your boat sit idle for a length of time.

Your engine needs to be "winterized." (What? Winterized in tropical Mexico?) This phrase means to follow your manufacturer's suggestions for intermittent engine usage in order to properly care for the engine.

For example, you must fly home for what was supposed to be two weeks and you are gone for an additional two. Although you have hired a Mexican to look after the boat, you have not given him the authority to run the engine or the boat. You return, try to start the engine—and nothing works. You have not done the necessary preventive maintenance to keep all mechanical parts functioning.

This lack of maintenance once you get to your final or interim destination is why so many boats make the run to Mexico so suc-cessfully and must make extensive repairs before returning to the States.

EMERGENCIES

If a member of the crew must leave and a replacement comes aboard, the ship's papers must be changed accordingly. You must visit the same list of officials as before. If the captain must return to the States and a new skipper takes over, the captain should go with this person to each offi-cial. If this is not possible (such as the skipper must leave over a weekend), he should write down the change of command and have it notarized, if at all possible. Should this be impossible, he should send a telegram stating the change of command to the Mexican Captain of the Port immediately upon his return to the U.S.

Should you have a boating disaster, DO NOT LEAVE YOUR BOAT UNATTENDED. As in any foreign country (and frequently in the U.S.), the boat will be stripped of anything of value in an extremely short period of time.

RETURNING TO THE U.S.

The yellow quarantine flag should be flown above the flag of the country you have just exited. If you arrive at U.S. Customs after hours, you may stay up to 24 hours without clearance as long as no one leaves the boat. If you are anxious to get home, you can call for an inspection officer who will charge you for this inconvenience.

U.S. Customs will ask where you have been, talk to each person aboard and inquire what was purchased and its value, collect the papers and, perhaps, search the vessel. The names on the crew list should agree with the names of those aboard.

Most fresh fruits and vegetables will be confiscated so eat your produce before you get back to the States.

Besides the words and phrases in this chapter, see Chapter 15, ENGINES AND TOOLS, and Chapter 16, ALL ABOUT NAVIGATION, for additional information.

TYPES OF BOATS

Is that a____?.............¿Ehs EH-soh____?
                    (¿Es éso____?)

```
boat...........................BOH-tay
              (bote, m)
    or.........................BAHR-kah
              (barca)
canoe.........................kah-NOH-ah
              (canoa)
    or.......................chah-LOO-pah
              (chalupa)
cruiser.....................kroo-SAY-roh
              (crucero)
cutter..........................KOO-tehr
              (cúter, m)
dingy..........................PAHN-gah
              (panga)
    or.........................DEEN-gay
              (dinghy)
dory...........................BOH-tay
              (bote, m)
ferryboat.............BAHR-koh day PAH-soh
            (barco de paso)
    or...............trahns-bohr-dah-DOHR
            (transbordador, m)
fleet..........................FLOH-tah
              (flota)
    or........................ahr-MAH-dah
              (armada)
freighter...................kahr-gah-DOHR
              (cargador, m)
junk..........................WHOON-koh
              (junco)
ketch..........................KAY-chay
              (queche, f)
launch........................LAHN-chah
              (lancha)
lifeboat.........BOH-tay sahl-bah-BEE-dahs
            (bote salvavidas)
motorboat............LAHN-chah moh-TOH-rah
            (lancha motora)
rowboat..............BOH-tay day RAY-mohs
            (bote de remos)
sabot.........................SWAY-koh
              (zueco)
```

```
sailboat...............BAHR-kah day BAY-lah
             (barca de vela)
   or......................bay-LAY-roh
             (velero)
schooner.....................goh-LAY-tah
             (goleta)
   or......................ehs-KOO-nah
             (escuna)
ship.............................NAH-bay
             (nave, f)
small craft
  ....ehm-bahr-kah-see-OHN-ays may-NOH-rays
         (embarcaciones menores)
speedboat...........LAHN-chah kah-RRAY-rahs
         (lancha carreras)
towboat, tugboat.........ray-mohl-kah-DOHR
         (remolcador, m)
yacht.............................YAH-tay
             (yate, m)
yawl.............................YOH-lay
             (yole, f)
```

CREW

```
I am a____................Yoh SOH-ee____.
         (Yo soy____.)
He (she) is a____.....Ehl (EH-yah) ehs____.
    (Él (ella) es____.)

boatman......................bahr-KAY-roh
             (barquero)
captain.......................kah-pee-TAHN
             (capitán, m)
cook..................koh-see-NAY-rah (-o)
         (cocinera, -o)
crew.................tree-poo-lah-see-OHN
             (tripulación)
crew member..............tree-poo-LAHN-tay
             (tripulante, m)
deck hand
   .....mah-ree-NAY-roh day koo-bee-EHR-tah
         (marinero de cubierto)
```

200

```
engineer...............een-hay-nee‑AY-roh
              (ingeniero)
helmsman...............tee-moh-NAY-roh
              (timonero)
mate or pilot..............pee-LOH-toh
              (piloto)
  or, mate.....say-GOON-doh day ah BOHR-doh
          (segundo de a bordo)
navigator..............nah-bay-GAHN-tay
              (navegante, m)
oarsman.....................ray-MAY-roh
              (remero)
rigger...............ah-pah-ray-hah-DOHR
              (aparejador, m)
sailor...................mah-ree-NAY-roh
              (marinero)
skipper.......................HAY-fay
              (jefe, m)
  or........................kah-pee-TAHN
              (capitán, m)


(the next two are not for the crew list!)
galley slave...............gah-lay-OH-tay
              (galeote, m)

landlubber
   ....mah-ree-NAY-roh day AH-gwah DOOL-say
        (marinero de agua dulce)


I need____...........Nay-say-SEE-toh____.
              (Necesito____.)
Do you have____?..¿Tee‑AY-nay oos-TEHD____?
          (¿Tiene ud.____?)

Where is____?........¿DOHN-day ehs-TAH____?
          (¿Dónde está____?)


The____does not work.
   ...........Noh foonk-see‑OH-nah____.
          (No funciona____.)
The____is leaking.
   ...........Ehs-TAH goh-tay‑AHN-doh____.
          (Está goteando____.)
```

```
Send someone to repair my____.
  ..MAHN-day ah ahl-gee-EHN ah ray-pah-RAHR
                mee____.
   (Mande a alguien a reparar mi____.)

Can I____here?.........¿PWAY-doh____ah-KEE?
         (¿Puedo____aquí?)
  ...anchor.....................ahn-KLAHR
                 (anclar)
  ...tie up......................ah-TAHR
                 (atar)
  ...stay.................ray-mah-nay-SEHR
              (remanecer)

Please____..............Fah-BOHR day____.
   ...bring in the line.
        ray-koh-HEHR lah LEE-nay-ah.
       (Favor de recoger la línea.)
   ...cast off...........day-sah-mah-RRAHR.
          (Favor de desamarrar.)
   ...grab the line.
         ah-SEER lah LEE-nay-ah.
        (Favor de asir la línea.)
   ...hang the fenders.
      kohl-GAHR lahs day-FEHN-sahs.
     (Favor de colgar las defensas.)
   ...haul in the anchor.
          ah-LAHR lah AHN-klah.
        (Favor de halar la ancla.)
   ...hoist the sails.
        lay-bahn-TAHR lahs BAY-lahs.
      (Favor de levantar las velas.)
   ...push us off.
          day-sah-trah-KAHR-nohs.
        (Favor de desatracarnos.)
   ...ready the mooring lines.
      pray-pah-RARH lahs LEE-nay-ahs
                ah-mah-RRAHR.
   (Favor de preparar las líneas amarrar.)
   ...tie the line.
         ah-mah-RRAHR lah LEE-nay-ah.
       (Favor de amarrar la línea.)
```

Go to___port (starboard).
    ...BAH-yah ahl bah-BOHR (ehs-tree-BOHR).
        (Vaya al babor (estribor).
Go straight ahead.....SEE-gah day-RAY-choh.
            (Siga derecho.)
Are we clear?........¿HAY-mohs pah-SAH-doh?
            (¿Hemos pasado?)
Is the anchor set?
    ....¿Hah koh-HEE-doh lah AHN-klah?
        (¿Ha cogido la ancla?)
What is happening?............¿Kay PAH-sah?
            (¿Qué pasa?)
What happened?...............¿Kay pah-SOH?
            (¿Qué pasó?)
¡*!?*¿....................¡Kah-RAHM-bah!
            (¡Caramba!)
Do you have a cold beer?
¿Tee⌃EH-nay oos-TEHD sehr-BAY-sah FREE⌃ah?
        (¿Tiene ud. cerveza fría?)

                AT THE BOAT YARD

Where is the boat yard?
    ¿DOHN-day ehs-TAH ehl ahs-tee-YAY-roh?
        (¿Dónde está el astillero?)

I need to haul out, to scrape, sand and
    paint the hull.

Nay-say-SEE-toh bah-RAHR, rahs-kay-tay⌃AHR,
    lee-HAHR ee peen-TAHR ehl KAHS-koh.
    ....(Necesito varar, rasquetear, lijar y
            pintar, el casco.)

I need a cradle.
    ..Nay-say-SEE-toh OO-nah KOO-nah PAH-rah
    ehl BAHR-koh.
    (Necesito una cuna para el barco.)

How much does it cost?
    ....¿KWAHN-toh KWEHS-tah?
            (¿Cuánto cuesta?)

When can you haul the boat?
........¿KWAHN-doh PWEH-day bah-RAHR-loh
ehl BAHR-koh?
(¿Cuándo puede vararlo el barco?)

At what time?...............¿Ah kay OH-rah?
(¿A qúe hora?)

(See Chapter 15 for parts, materials and
workmen.)

VOCABULARY

abeam..........................ah-trah-BAYS
(através)
aboard.........................ah BOHR-doh
(a bordo)
aft............................POH-pah
(popa)
ahead............ah-BAHN-tay pohr PROH͡ah
(avante por proa)
ahoy.....................ah dehl BAHR-koh
(a del barco)
air conditioning
......EYE-ray ah-kohn-dee-see͡ohn-AH-doh
(aire (m) acondicionado)
aloft..........................ah-RREE-bah
(arriba)
amidships....ehn MAY-dee͡oh dehl nah-BEE͡oh
(en medio del navío)
anchor.........................AHN-klah
(ancla)
   bolt.......tohr-NEE-yoh day ahn-KLAH-hay
(tornillo de anclaje)
   chocks............KAHL-sohs day AHN-klah
(calzos de ancla)
   drag..........AHN-klah day ah-RRAHS-tray
(ancla de arrastre)
   fees......day-RAY-chohs day ahn-KLAH-hay
(derechos de anclaje)
   flukes.............OO-nyahs day AHN-klah
(uñas de ancla)

kedge......................ahn-KLOH-tay
       (anclote, m)
  line..........KWEHR-dah day lah AHN-klah
     (cuerda de la ancla)
  nut.............oh-RAY-hah day AHN-klah
      (oreja de ancla)
  shaft.............KAH-nyah day AHN-klah
      (caña de ancla)
  tripper...............dees-pah-rah-DOHR
      (disparador)
at anchor....................ahl HOOS-tay
      (al juste)
  to anchor....................ahn-KLAHR
      (anclar)
anchorage....................ahn-KLAH-hay
      (anclaje, m)
  to ride at anchor.........dahr FOHN-doh
      (dar fondo)
  sea anchor........AHN-klah floh-TAHN-tay
     (ancla flotante)
  to weigh anchor..............sahr-PAHR
      (zarpar)
backstay..........................BOOR-dah
      (burda)
  or......................brahn-DAH-lays
     (brandales, m)
ballast..........................LAHS-tray
      (lastre, m)
batten............................LAH-tah
      (lata)
  or........................lees-TOHN
     (listón, m)
  to batten....tah-PAHR kohn lees-TOH-nays
     (tapar con listones)
to beach.........................bah-RAHR
      (varar)
beam.........................pahn-TOH-kay
      (pantoque, m)
  (structural).....................BEE-gah
      (viga)
to becalm.......................kahl-MAHR
      (calmar)

```
berth (bunk)...................LEE-tay-rah
                (lítera)
bilge..........................pahn-TOH-kay
                (pantoque, m)
  pumps.........BOHM-bahs day kah-RAY-nah
           (bombas de carena)
  water..........AH-gwah day pahn-TOH-kay
           (agua de pantoque)
block............................moh-TOHN
                (motón, m)
to board.......................ah-bohr-DAHR
                (abordar)
boat hook......................bee-CHAY-roh
                (bichero)
boat race......................ray-GAH-tah
                (regata)
boat yard...................ahs-tee-YAY-roh
                (astillero)
bobstay....................bahr-bee-KAY-hoh
                (barbiquejo)
boom.......................boh-tah-BAH-rah
                (botavara)
  sail..............BAY-lah kahn-GRAY-hah
           (vela cangreja)
bosuns chair.....................BAHL-soh
                (balso)
bow.............................PROH-ah
                (proa)
bowsprit.......................baow-PREHS
                (bauprés, m)
broadside.....................kohs-TAH-doh
                (costado)
bulkhead......................mahm-PAH-roh
                (mamparo)
bulwark.....................ah-moo-RAH-dah
                (amurada)
bunk.......................kah-mah-ROH-tay
                (camarote, m)
cabin.........................kah-BEE-nah
                (cabina)
capstan................kah-brehs-TAHN-tay
                (cabrestante, m)
```

to careen....................een-klee-NAHR
                (inclinar)
centerboard.........................OHR-sah
                (orza)
    or......................sehn-tree-BOHRD
                (centribord, m)
chain........................kah-DAY-nah
                (cadena)
chainplate..................kah-day-NOH-tay
                (cadenote, m)
chock............................CHOH-kay
                (choque, m)
cleat.........................kohr-NOO-sah
                (cornuza)
    or.................ah-brah-sah-DAY-rah
                (abrazadera)
clew.................POO-nyoh day BAY-lah
                (puño de vela)
closehauled........bahr-loh-behn-tay⁀AH-doh
                (barloventeado)
Coast Guard.........GWAHR-dah day KOHS-tahs
                (guarda de costas)
cockpit.........................bah-NAY-rah
                (banera)
companionway
    ....ehs-kah-LAY-rah day KAH-mah-rah
            (escalera de cámara)
    or......................ehs-koh-TEE-yah
                (escotilla)
cradle.............................KOOH-nah
                (cuna)
crows nest...KOH-fah PAH-rah lah bee-HEE⁀ah
            (cofa para la vigía)
cruise................bee⁀AH-hay pohr mahr
                (viaje por mar)
    to cruise.......................bah-GAHR
                (vagar)
    or......................nah-bay-GAHR
                (navegar)
cruising speed
    ....bay-loh-see-DAHD day kroo-SAY-roh
            (velocidad de crusero)

```
Customs........................ah-DWAH-nah
                  (aduana)
davit............pehs-KAHN-tay day BOH-tay
            (pescante de bote)
deck.......................koo-bee-EHR-tah
                  (cubierta)
  on deck........SOH-bray koo-bee-EHR-tah
            (sobre cubierta)
deckhouse..........kah-mah-RAY-tah AHL-tah
            (camareta alta)
depth...................proh-foon-dee-DAHD
                  (profundidad, f)
  or...........................poon-TAHL
                  (puntal, m)
to dismast...............dees-ahr-boh-LAHR
                  (disarbolar)
dock..............................DEE-kay
                  (dique, m)
dockage (docking).ehn-TRAH-dah ehn MUAY-yay
            (entrada en muelle)
docking fee...................muay-YAH-hay
                  (muellaje, m)
dolphin striker.....MOH-koh dehl baow-PREHS
            (moco del bauprés)
draft.........................kah-LAH-doh
                  (calado)
duffel bag.....................tah-LAY-goh
                  (talego)
fastening...........ehn-kah-pee-yah-DOO-rah
            (encapilladura)
to fend off...................ray-chah-SAHR
                  (rechazar)
fender.......................day-FEHN-sahs
                  (defensas)
flag..........................bahn-DAY-rah
                  (bandera)
to float........................floh-TAHR
                  (flotar)
floating dock.........DEE-kay floh-TAHN-tay
            (dique (m) flotante)
floor timbers................bah-REHN-gahs
                  (varengas)
```

```
fore and aft.........day POH-pah ah PROH⌃ah
            (de popa a proa)
forecastle...................kahs-TEE-yoh
            (castillo)
foredeck........koo-bee⌃EHR-tah day PROH⌃ah
            (cubierta de proa)
foremast.........PAH-loh day treen-KAY-tay
            (palo de trinquete)
forepeak.........................rah-SEHL
            (racel, m)
or..............dehl-GAH-doh day PROH⌃ah
            (delgado de proa)
forestay..............ehs-TAY day PROH⌃ah
            (estay de proa)
forestay sail............treen-kay-TEE-yah
            (trinquetilla)
frame......................kwah-DEHR-nah
            (cuaderna)
freeboard.................OH-brah MWEHR-tah
            (obra muerta)
fresh water...............AH-gwah DOOL-say
            (agua (m) dulce)
full sail..................BAY-lah YAY-nah
            (vela llena)
full stop.................POON-toh fee-NAHL
            (punto final)
gaff.........................gahr-FEE⌃oh
            (garfío)
  boom.........BEHR-gah day kahn-GRAY-hah
            (verga de cangreja)
    spar.....................kahn-GRAY-hah
            (cangreja)
      or...................boh-tah-BAH-rah
            (botavara)
galley........................gah-LAY-rah
            (galera)
gangplank.......................PLAHN-chah
            (plancha)
garboard.............ah-pah-rah-DOO-rah
            (aparadura)
```

garboard strake
........tah-BLOHN day ah-pah-rah-DOO-rah
         (tablón de aparadura)

genoa jib.....................hay-noh-BAYS
              (genovés, m)
gooseneck.SOON-choh day lah boh-tah-BAH-rah
         (zuncho de la botavara)
grommet.............ehs-TROH-boh ah-MOO-rah
         (estrobo amura)
gunnel..........................ray-GAH-lah
                (regala)
    or............................BOHR-dah
                (borda)
halyard.........................DREE-sah
                (driza)
hammock.......................ah-MAH-kah
                (hamaca)
handrail..................PAH-sah-MAH-noh
                (pasamano)
hatch.....................ehs-koh-TEE-yah
                (escotilla)
to haul (change course)............bee-RAHR
                (virar)
to haul out......................bah-RAHR
                (varar)
hawse holes...................ehs-koh-BEHN
                (escobén, m)
hawse pipes
    ..boh-SEE-nahs day lohs ehs-koh-BEHN-ays
        (bocinas de los escobenes)
head........................day PROH^ah
                (de proa)
    or......................ehs-koo-SAH-doh
                (escusado)
headsail..........BAY-lah day lahn-TAY-rah
         (vela de lantera)
heater..................kah-lehn-tah-DOHR
                (calentador, m)
to heel......................ehs-koh-RAHR
                (escorar)

helm.............................tee-MOHN
              (timón, m)
   or..........................KAH-nyah
              (caña)
to hoist.....................lay-bahn-TAHR
              (levantar)
hold (the).....................boh-DAY-gah
              (bodega)
hull...........................KAHS-koh
              (casco)
ice............................YAY-loh
              (heilo)
ice box......................nay-BAY-rah
              (nevera)
immigration...............mee-grah-see-OHN
              (migración)
in irons..........PROH-ah ehn-kahn-TAH-dah
            (proa encantada)
jib...............................FOH-kay
              (foque, m)
   boom...............BRAH-soh day GROO-ah
              (brazo de grua)
to jibe....................trahs-loo-CHAHR
              (trasluchar)
to kedge......ah-LAHR pohr ehl ahn-KLOH-tay
          (halar por el anclote)
keel...........................KEE-yah
              (quilla)
keelson....................soh-bray-KEE-yah
              (sobrequilla)
knees..........................KOOR-bah
              (curva)
lashing......................ah-MAH-rrah
              (amarra)
latch......................pehs-TEE-yoh
              (pestillo)
lateen sail............BAY-lah lah-TEE-nah
              (vela latina)
lazarette..................lah-sah-RAY-toh
              (lazareto)
lead line.................ehs-kahn-DAH-yoh
              (escandallo)

211

```
leak....................ah-SEHR AH-gwah
              (hacer agua)
leaving port..................sah-LEE-dah
              (salida)
lee.....................soh-tah-BEHN-tay
              (sotavente, m)
   shore......KOHS-tah day soh-tah-BEHN-tay
           (costa de sotavente)
   side.......BAHN-dah day soh-tah-BEHN-tay
           (banda de sotavente)
leeboards.................ohr-sah-DAY-rahs
              (orzaderas)
leeward................ah soh-tah-BEHN-toh
              (a sotavento)
leeway.......................day-REE-bah
              (deriva)
life line........KAH-blay sahl-bah-BEE-dahs
           (cable salvavidas)
life preservers...........sahl-bah-BEE-dahs
              (salvavidas)
line (rope)....................LEE-nay^ah
              (línea)
locker..........................roh-PAY-roh
              (ropero)
log book..kwah-DEHR-noh day bee-TAH-koh-rah
           (cuaderno de bitácora)
luff...........................grah-TEEL
              (gratil)
main stay................ehs-TAY mah-YOHR
              (estay major)
mainmast..............PAH-loh day mah-YOHR
           (palo de major)
mainsail.................BAY-lah mah-YOHR
              (vela major)
man overboard.........OHM-bray ahl AH-gwah
           (hombre al agua)
maritime insurance
    ........say-GOO-roh day mah-REE-tee-moh
           (seguro de marítimo)
maritime law....KOH-dee-goh mah-REE-tee-moh
           (código marítimo)
```

```
mast.............................PAH-loh
                (palo)
masthead.............TOH-pay day mahs-TEEL
          (tope (m) de mastil)
mizzen mast........PAH-loh day may-SAH-noh
          (palo de mesano)
mizzen sail...................may-SAH-nah
                (mesana)
mizzen shrouds..HAHR-see-ah day may-SAH-nah
          (jarcia de mesana)
mizzen topsail........soh-bray-may-SAH-nah
                (sobremesana)
nautical......................NOW-tee-koh
                (náutico)
night watch...................say-RAY-noh
                (sereno)
oar..............................RAY-moh
                (remo)
   to oar or row..................ray-MAHR
                (remar)
oarlock...................choo-may-SAY-rah
                (chumacera)
offshore................mahr ah-FWAY-rah
                (mar afuera)
on shore.................ehn lah KOHS-tah
                (en la costa)
outboard motor
   .........moh-TOHR FWAY-rah day BOHR-dah
       (motor (m) fuera de borda)
outrigger.....................ohr-KAY-tah
                (horqueta)
overboard.........................ahl mahr
                (al mar)
overhaul.............ray-pah-rah-see-OHN
          (reparación, f)
paddle..........................PAH-lah
                (pala)
padlock.....................kahn-DAH-doh
                (candado)
peak halyard.........DREE-sah dehl PEE-koh
                (driza del pico)
```

```
plank............................tah-BLOHN
                 (tablón, f)
port (left)......................bah-BOHR
                 (babor, m)
Port Captains Office.....kah-pee-tah-NEE-ah
                 (capitanía)
porthole...................klah-rah-BOH-yah
                 (claraboya)
propeller........................AY-lee-say
                 (hélice, m)
   or..........................proh-PAY-lah
                 (propela)
prow.............................PROH-ah
                 (proa)
pump.............................BOHM-bah
                 (bomba)
reaching................dehs-kwahr-TAHR
                 (descuartar)
reef points......................REE-sohs
                 (rizos)
   to reef.............toh-MAHR oon REE-soh
                 (tomar un rizo)
refrigerator..........ray-free-hee-rah-DOHR
                 (refrigerador, m)
to refuel....................ray-pohs-TAHR
                 (repostar)
ribs....................kohs-tee-YAH-hay
                 (costillaje, m)
right of way......day-RAY-choh dehl PAH-soh
                 (derecho del paso)
rigging..................ah-pahr-RAY-hoh
                 (aparejo, m)
   to rig................ehn-kah-pee-YAHR
                 (encapillar)
rope..........................HAHR-see-ah
                 (jarcia)
   or.........................kohr-DAH-hay
                 (cordaje)
rudder...........................tee-MOHN
                 (timón, m)
running.............bee-EHN-toh ehn POH-pah
                 (viento en popa)
```

safety belt.seen-too-ROHN sahl-bah-BEE-dahs
(cinturón salvavidas)

sail.................................BAY-lah
(vela)

to sail.........................sah-LEER
(salir)

or......................nah-bay-GAHR
(navegar)

sail loft....................teen-GLAH-doh
(tinglado)

sail yard........................BEHR-gah
(verga)

sailable..................nah-bay-GAH-blay
(navegable)

sailing...............nah-bay-gah-see-OHN
(navegación, f)

sailing directions
........noh-TEE-see-ahs mah-REE-tee-mahs
(noticias marítimas)

salvage..................sahl-bah-MEHN-toh
(salvamento)

scantlings....................bah-RROH-tays
(barrotes)

scupper......................eem-bohr-NAHL
(imbornal, m)

sea..................................mahr
(mar, m or f)

at sea....................ehn ehl mahr
(en el mar)

searchlight................ray-flehk-TOHR
(reflector, m)

seasick....................mah-ray-AH-doh
(mareado)

seawater..................AH-gwah day mahr
(agua (m) de mar)

seaway.............ROO-tah mah-REE-tee-mah
(ruta marítima)

set of oars...........WHAY-goh day RAY-mohs
(juego de remos)

to set sail.........ah-SEHR-say ah-lah-MAHR
(hacerse alamar)

215

```
shackle.......................gree-YAY-tay
             (grillete, m)
   or............................TRAH-bah
             (traba)
shackle bolt.KAHN-kah-moh dehl gree-YAY-tay
   (cáncamo del grillete)
sheet.........................ehs-KOH-tah
             (escota)
shipboard.......................BOHR-doh
             (bordo)
ships papers......pah-PAY-lays lay-GAH-lays
             (papeles legales)
shipshape...............ehn bwehn OHR-dehn
             (en buen orden)
shipwreck..................now-FRAH-heeˆoh
             (naufragio)
shower..........................DOO-chah
             (ducha)
shrouds.....................oh-BEHN-kays
             (obenques, f)
   or........................HAHR-seeˆahs
             (jarcias)
slack (ropes)..........KAH-bohs SWEHL-tohs
             (cabos sueltos)
small boom.................boh-tah-BAH-rah
             (botavara)
sounding.....................sohn-DAYˆoh
             (sondeo)
   lead...................ehs-kahn-DAH-yoh
             (escandallo)
   line...................sohn-dah-LAY-sah
             (sondaleza)
spar............................BEHR-gah
             (verga)
spinnaker.......................bah-LOHN
             (balón, m)
   or............BAY-lah treeˆahn-goo-LAHR
             (vela triangular)
spinnaker pole......tahn-GOHN dehl bah-LOHN
         (tangon (m) del balón)
spot light......................FOH-koh
             (foco)

                216
```

```
stanchion.................kahn-day-LAY-roh
            (candelero)
starboard....................ehs-tree-BOHR
            (estribor, m)
stay.............................ehs-TAY
            (estay, m)
staysail..............BAY-lah day ehs-TAY
            (vela de estay)
steering wheel...............boh-LAHN-tay
            (volante, m)
stem............................ROH-dah
            (roda)
to step a mast.....plahn-TAHR oon MAHS-teel
            (plantar un mástil)
stern...........................POH-pah
            (popa)
stern timbers.....gahm-BOH-tays day POH-pah
            (gambotes de popa)
sternpost.....................koh-DAHS-tay
            (codaste, m)
sternway..........................SEE⌃ah
            (cía)
storm sail............tah-yah-bee⌃EHN-tohs
            (tallavientos)
stove.........................ehs-TOO-fah
            (estufa)
stowage.......................ehs-TEE-bah
            (estiba)
   to stow....................ehs-tee-BAHR
            (estibar)
strut........................ehs-pah-LOHN
            (espalón)
tack...........................ah-MOO-rah
            (amura)
   to tack.......................bee-RAHR
            (virar)
tackle.....................ah-pah-RAY-hoh
            (aparejo)
taffrail...........koh-roh-nah-mee⌃EHN-toh
            (coronamiento)
tank...........................TAHN-kay
            (tanque, m)
```

throat halyards......DREE-sahs dehl FOH-kay
(drisas de foque)

throttle...................ray-goo-lah-DOHR
(regulador, m)

tiller.............................KAH-nyah
(caña)

   or.............................tee-MOHN
(timón, m)

   chain........................gwahr-DEEN
(guardín, m)

   holes.......................lee-MAY-rah
(limera)

toe rail.proh-tehk-TOHR day koo-bee^EHR-tah
(protector de cubierta)

ton........................toh-nay-LAH-dah
(tonelada)

tonnage...................toh-nay-LAH-hay
(tonelaje, m)

top mast..................mahs-tay-LAY-roh
(mastelero)

topsail........................GAH-bee^ah
(gavia)

topsail sheets............ehs-koh-TEE-nays
(escotines, m)

topside...........................BOHR-dah
(borda)

tow............................ray-MOHL-kay
(remolque)

   to tow....................ray-mohl-KAHR
(remolcar)

tow line..........KAH-blay day ray-MOHL-kay
(cable de remolque)

transom................PAY-toh day POH-pah
(peto de popa)

to trim the sails...........oh-ree^ehn-TAHR
(orientar)

trysail..............BAY-lah kahn-GRAY-hah
(vela cangreja)

turnbuckle.................tohr-nee-KAY-tay
(torniquete, m)

under full sail..........ah TOH-dah BAY-lah
(a toda vela)

```
watch........................GWAHR-dee⌃ah
               (guardia)
water............................AH-gwah
               (agua, m)
water line..........LEE-nay⌃ah day AH-gwah
               (línea de agua)
water heater..kah-lehn-tah-DOHR day AH-gwah
            (calentador de agua)
water tank........TAHN-kay PAH-rah AH-gwah
            (tanque (f) para agua)
weatherboard.......LAH-doh dehl bee⌃EHN-toh
            (lado del viento)
wheel..............roo⌃AY-dah dehl tee-MOHN
            (rueda del timón)
windlass, winch.........mohn-tah-KAHR-gahs
            (montacargas)
   or.............................TOHR-noh
               (torno)
windshield..............PAH-rah-BREE-sahs
            (parabrisas)
windward..............ah bahr-loh-BEHN-toh
            (a barlovento)
yaw......................ghee-NYAH-dah
               (guiñada)
   to yaw.......................ghee-NYAHR
               (guiñar)
```

DIVING GEAR

```
diver...............................BOO-soh
                (buzo)
    or......................boo-say-ah-DOHR
              (buceador, m)
fins...........................ah-LAY-tahs
                (aletas)
gloves.........................GWAHN-tays
               (guantes)
mask..............................BEE-soh
                (viso)
regulator.................ray-goo-lah-DOHR
              (regulador, m)
scuba tank..........TAHN-kay day boo-SAY-oh
             (tanque de buceo)
snorkle........................ay-NOHR-kay
               (enorke, m)
spear gun............pees-TOH-lah dehl mahr
              (pistola del mar)
weight belt.......seen-too-ROHN day PAY-soh
             (cinturón de peso)
wet suit............TRAH-hay day boo-SAY-oh
             (traje (m) de buceo)
```

Repairs and Servicing

CARAMBA!

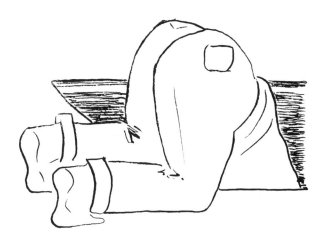

Before you leave the States, pack important
spares for your mode of transportation:
fuel filters, water pumps, gaskets, clamps
impellors, epoxy glue, etc. If something
does break, first check with other Americans in the area to see if they brought
along the tool or part you require. Frequently, in lieu of money, exchanges of
similarly priced parts or a trade-off of
skills are all that are necessary to get
what you need.

Mexican stores do not carry large inventories. Vehicle parts are easier to obtain than items for a boat or aircraft engine; however, do not discredit the ingenuity of Mexican technicians to jury-rig with items on hand and come up with a temporary solution to the problem. On a trip up from Puerto Vallarta, we needed a part for a Perkins diesel. Naturally, such an item was not available but a make-shift part that worked splendidly for the rest of the voyage was created by using tractor parts.

If the part cannot be duplicated or repaired, probably the least expensive way to get the part--and to make sure you get the part economically and on a timely basis--is to have someone from the States take the bus or fly down with the item.

One other item needs mentioning--<u>mordida.</u> Mordida, "the bite," or a little money under the table, is just as common for expediting a situation in Mexico as it is anywhere else. It is frequently used to speed up paper work for an exit if you have been in port several months, for bringing in items that are not considered for personal use, such as major engine replacement parts and so forth.

Whenever possible, take the broken piece or part requiring repair with you. This eliminates lengthy, sometimes stumbling explanations. If you cannot do so, then link together the necessary vocabulary words to express your desires. For example:

I need a hose clamp for the engine.

I need--.................Nay-say-SEE-toh---
               (Necesito--)
  a hose clamp--.........................
          (literally, a clamp for the hose)
     ....OO-nah ah-brah-sah-DAY-rah day
              lah mahn-GWAY-rah---
      (una abrazadera de la manguera--)
     for the engine....PAH-rah ehl moh-TOHR.
              (para el motor.)

  (Necesito una abrazadera de la manguera
              para el motor.)

I need to borrow____.
     ....Nay-say-SEE-toh prehs-TAHR____.
          (Necesito prestar____.)

It needs new____.
   ...Nay-say-SEE-tah NWAY-bohs (-ahs)____.
       (Necesita nuevos (-as)____.)
----is broken.............Say kay-BROH____.
          (Se quebró____.)
It does not work.............Noh SEER-bay.
              (No sirve.)
Do you have____?..¿Tee-AY-nay oos-TEHD____?
          (¿Tiene ud.____?)
Where can I buy____?
     ......¿DOHN-day PWAY-day kohm-PRAHR____?
        (¿Dónde puede comprar____?)
How much does it cost?
     ....KWAHN-toh KWEHS-tah?
            (¿Cuánto cuesta?)
Fill up____...................YAY-nay____.
              (Llene____.)
Change____................KAHM-bee-ay____.
              (Cambie____.)
Examine (check)____...Eggs-SAH-mee-nay____.
              (Examine____.)
Look at____...............Ray-BEE-say____.
              (Revise____.)

223

I want the____changed.
............Kee-AIR-oh kahm-bee-AHR____.
          (Quiero cambiar____.)
I want it greased.
..........Kee-AIR-oh ehn-grah-SAHR-loh.
          (Quiero engrasarlo.)

Please____ the____........Fah-BOHR day____.
              (Favor de____.)
...adjust the brakes.
          ....ah-hoos-TAHR lohs FRAY-nohs.
          (Favor de ajustar los frenos.)
...change the oil.
          ....kahm-bee-AHR ehl ah-SAY-tay.
          (Favor de cambiar el aceite.)
...check the oil.
          ....behr ehl ah-SAY-tay.
          (Favor de ver el aceite.)
...lubricate____......loo-bree-KAHR____.
          (Favor de lubricar____.)
...wash____................lah-BAHR____.
          (Favor de lavar____.)
...tighten the brakes.
          ....ah-pray-TAHR lohs FRAY-nohs.
          (Favor de apretar los frenos.)
...tune the engine.
          ..poh-NEHR ahl POON-toh ehl moh-TOHR.
          (Favor de poner al punto el motor.)

It has a knock.
          ......Tee-AY-nay oon dehs-pehr-FEHK-toh.
                (Tiene un desperfecto.)
It is not running properly.
          .....Ehl moh-TOHR noh MAHR-chah bee-EHN.
          (El motor no marcha bien.)

The battery is dead.
          Lah bah-tay-REE-ah noh foon-see-OH-nah.
                (La batería no funciona.)
Put water in the battery.
          POHN-gah AH-gwah ehn lah bah-tay-REE-ah.
                (Ponga agua en la batería.)

The battery needs charging.
......Lah bah-tay-REE⌃ah nay-say-SEE-tah
KAHR-gah.
(La batería necesita carga.)

The gas line is clogged.
..Lah too-behr-EE⌃ah day gah-soh-LEE-nah
ehs-TAH tah-PAH-dah.
(La tubería de gasolina está tapada.)

The clutch slips.
.........Ehl ehm-BRAH-gay rehs-BAHL-dah.
(El embrague resbalda.)

Can you fix it?
...¿PWAY-day oohs-TEHD ray-pah-RAHR-loh?
(¿Puede ud. repararlo?)
How long will it take to fix?
........¿KWAHN-toh tee⌃EHM-poh toh-mah-RAH
PAH-rah ray-pah-RAHR-loh?
(¿Cuánto tiempo tomará para repararlo?)
We can (not) fix it.
....(Noh) Poh-DAY-mohs ray-pah-RAHR-loh.
(No) Podemos repararlo.)
We have (not) the right parts.
(Noh) Tay-NAY-mohs lohs ahk-seh-SOH-ree⌃ohs
koh-REHS-pohn-dee⌃EHN-tays.
(No) Tenemos los accesorios
correspondientes.)

We have to send for them.
........Tay-NAY-mohs kay mahn-DAHR-lohs.
(Tenemos que mandarlos.)

I can fix it temporarily.
......PWAY-doh ray-pah-RAHR-loh pohr ehl
moh-MEHN-toh.
(Puedo repararlo por el momento.)

How much do I owe you?
................¿KWAHN-toh lay DAY-boh?
(¿Cuánto le debo?)

ENGINES

accelerator..............ah-say-lay-RAH-doh
           (acelerado)
accessory..............ahk-seh-SOH-ree^ohs
           (accesorios)
to adjust.....................ah-hoos-TAHR
           (ajustar)
ampere......................ahm-PAY-ree^oh
           (amperio)
amperemeter...........ahm-pay-REE-may-troh
           (amperímetro)
asbestos.....................ahs-BEHS-toh
           (asbesto)
auxiliary..............ah-dee-see^oh-NAHL
           (adicional)
ball bearing..................bah-LAY-roh
           (balero)
battery....................bah-tay-REE^ah
           (batería)
   or............................PEE-lah
           (pila)
   dry.........bah-tay-REE^ah day PEE-lahs
          (batería de pilas)
   to charge a battery
      ......kahr-GAHR OO-nah bah-tay-REE^ah
          (cargar una batería)
bearing....................koh-hee-NAY-tay
           (cojinete, m)
belt.......................seen-too-ROHN
           (cinturón, f)
   or............................BAHN-dah
           (banda)
bracket......................MEHN-soo-lah
           (ménsula)
butane.......................boo-TAH-noh
           (butano)
cable...........................KAH-blay
           (cable, m)
cam shaft............AHR-bohl day LAY-bahs
          (árbol (m) de levas)

226

carburetor................kahr-boo-rah-DOHR
(carburador, m)
choke...........................EYE-ray
(aire, m)
circuit breaker.......KOHR-toh seer-KEE-toh
(corto circuito)
clamp...........................GRAH-pah
(grapa)
clutch........................ehm-BRAH-gay
(embrague, m)
   to engage the clutch.......ehm-brah-GAHR
(embragar)
coaxial....................koh^ahks-ee^AHL
(coaxial, m)
coil............................boh-BEEN
(bobbin, f)
compressor..................kohm-pray-SOHR
(compresor, m)
condenser...............kohn-dehn-sah-DOHR
(condensador, m)
conduit..........................TOO-boh
(tubo)
connecting rod..................bee^AY-lah
(biela)
converter...............kohn-behr-tee-DOHR
(convertidor, m)
coolant
   ah-HEHN-tay day ray-free-hay-rah-see^OHN
(agente (m) de refrigeración)
cotter pin....................chah-BAY-tah
(chaveta)
   or..........................YAH-bay
(llave, f)
crankcase......KAHR-tehr day see-gway-NYAHL
(cárter (m) de cigueñal)
crankshaft..................see-gway-NYAHL
(cigueñal, m)
current meter
   .....kohn-tah-DOHR day een-tehn-see-DAHD
(contador de intensidad)
cylinder.....................see-LEEN-droh
(cilindro)

227

```
diesel........................dee-SEHL
              (diesel, m)
differential.....................MAH-sah
              (maza)
diode..........................dee-OH-doh
              (diodo)
to disconnect...........dehs-koh-nehk-TAHR
              (disconectar)
distilled water....AH-gwah dehs-tee-LAH-dah
              (agua destilada)
distributor.........dees-tree-bwee-ah-DOHR
              (distribuiador, m)
driving shaft........AHR-bohl day moh-TOHR
              (árbol (m) de motor)
dry cell....................PEE-lah SAY-kah
              (pila seca)
electric...................ay-LEHK-tree-koh
              (eléctrico)
electricity..........ay-lehk-tree-see-DAHD
              (electricidad, f)
electrolysis.........ay-lehk-TROH-lee-sees
              (electrólisis f)
electronics............ay-lehk-TROH-nee-kah
              (electrónica)
engine........................MAH-kee-nah
              (máquina)
   or............................moh-TOHR
              (motor, m)
engine pin.....................kah-BEE-yah
              (cabilla)
exhaust.......................ehs-KAH-pay
              (escape, m)
expansion valve
      .......BAHL-boo-lah day eks-pahn-see-OHN
              (válvula de expansión)
fan....................behn-tee-lah-DOHR
              (ventilador, m)
fan belt...koh-RRAY-ah day behn-tee-LAH-doh
              (correa de ventilado)
filter..........................FEEL-troh
              (filtro)
```

```
fireproof.............een-kohm-boos-TEE-blay
                (incombustible)
flywheel.....................boh-LAHN-tay
                (volante, m)
fuel...................kohm-boos-TEE-blay
                (combustible, m)
fuse........................foo-SEE-blay
                (fusible, m)
gasket........................ehm-PAH-kay
                (empaque, m)
gasoline..................gah-soh-LEE-nah
                (gasolina)
gauge.....................een-dee-kah-DOHR
                (indicador, m)
gear...............roo-AY-dah dehn-TAH-dah
                (rueda de dentada)
   adjustment..bay-loh-see-DAHD KAHM-bee-oh
                (velocidad cambio)
   box............KAH-hah day KAHM-bee-ohs
                (caja de cambios)
   high...........................AHL-toh
                   (alto)
   low........................pree-MAY-roh
                   (primero)
   out of gear........day-sehm-brah-GAH-doh
                (desembragado)
   reverse..............MAHR-chah ah-TRAHS
                (marcha atrás)
   starting
      ....ehn-grah-NAH-hay day ah-RRAHN-kay
           (engranaje de arranque)
   system.................ehn-grah-NAH-hay
                (engranaje, m)
   to put into gear...ah-SEHR ehn-grah-NAHR
                (hacer engranar)
   to shift gears.............kahm-bee-AHR
                (cambiar)
gearshift........PLAHN-kah day KAHM-bee-ohs
                (planca de cambios)
generator.................hay-nah-rah-DOHR
                (generador, m)
```

```
grease.........................GRAH-sah
              (grasa)
   to grease.................ehn-grah-SAHR
              (engrasar)
heater...................kah-lehn-tah-DOHR
              (calentador, m)
heavy duty...day grahn ray-sees-TEHN-see-ah
          (de gran resistencia)
horsepower.......kah-BAH-yoh day FWEHR-sah
          (caballo de fuerza)
hose..........................mahn-GAY-rah
              (manguera)
   clamp................ah-brah-sah-DAY-ran
              (abrazadera)
hydraulic..................ee-DRAUW-lee-koh
              (hidráulico)
idler.....................roo-AY-dah LOH-kah
              (rueda loca)
ignition...................ehn-sehn-DEE-doh
              (encendido)
   or........................eeg-nee-see-OHN
              (ignición, f)
impellor.....................eem-pool-SOHR
              (impulsor, m)
indicator..................een-dee-kah-DOHR
              (indicador, m)
induction coil................kah-RRAY-tay
              (carrete, m)
injector......................een-yehk-TOHR
              (inyector, m)
installation...........eens-tah-lah-see-OHN
              (instalación, f)
   to install................eens-tah-LAHR
              (instalar)
instrument..............eens-troo-MEHN-toh
              (instrumento)
kerosene...................kay-roh-SEE-nah
              (kerosina)
key...............................YAH-bay
              (llave, f)
lubricant................loo-bree-KAHN-tay
              (lubricante, m)
```

230

```
lubrication............loo-bree-kah-see-OHN
            (lubricación, f)
   to lubricate..............loo-bree-KAHR
              (lubricar)
machine........................MAH-kee-nah
              (máquina)
manifold.....................MOOL-tee-play
              (múltiple, m)
mechanical.................may-KAH-nee-koh
              (mecánico)
mechanism.................may-kah-NEES-moh
              (mecanismo)
motor............................moh-TOHR
              (motor, m)
muffler..........................MOH-flay
              (mofle, m)
oil.............................ah-SAY-tay
              (aceite, m)
   to oil....................loo-bree-KAHR
              (lubricar)
     or........................ah-say-TAHR
              (aceitar)
to overhaul...................ray-pah-RAHR
              (reparar)
pipe..............................TOO-boh
              (tubo)
piston..........................pees-TOHN
              (pistón, m)
points.........................PLAH-tohs
              (platos)
propane.......................proh-PAH-noh
              (propano)
pump.............................BOHM-bah
              (bomba)
radiator...................rah-dee-ah-DOHR
              (radiador, m)
to recharge..................ray-kahr-GAHR
              (recargar)
refrigeration......ray-free-hay-rah-see-OHN
            (refrigeración, f)
refrigerant..........ray-free-hay-RAHN-tay
            (refrigerante, m)
```

```
to repair....................ray-pah-RAHR
                (reparar)
shaft........................FLAY-chah
                (flecha)
short circuit........KOHR-toh seer-KEE-toh
            (corto circuito)
socket (electric)......ray-sehp-TAH-koo-loh
            (receptáculo)
spare parts................ray-PWAYS-tohs
                (repuestos)
spark plug....................boo-HEE⌃ah
                (bujía)
speedometer...........bay-loh-SEE-may-troh
                (velocímetro)
spring (spiral)..............ray-SOHR-tay
                (resorte, m)
starter......................MAHR-chah
                (marcha)
switch.......................ehs-WEETCH
                (eswitch, m)
throttle................ray-goo-lah-DOHR
                (regulador, m)
thrust......................ehm-POO-hay
                (empuje, m)
to tighten...................ah-pray-TAHR
                (apretar)
to time the engine
    ......poh-NEHR ahl POON-toh ehl moh-TOHR
        (poner al punto el motor)
toggle switch...........een-tay-rroop-TOHR
                (interruptor)
torque.......ehs-FWEHR-soh day tohr-see⌃OHN
            (esfuerzo de torsión)
transmission...........trahns-mee-see⌃OHN
            (transmission, f)
valve.......................BAH-boo-lah
                (vávula)
    safety..BAH-boo-lah day say-goo-ree-DAHD
        (vávula de seguridad)
water heater..kah-lehn-tah-DOHR day AH-gwah
        (calentador (m) de agua)
```

watt........................BAH-tee^oh
                (vatio)

TOOLS

awl........................ah-REES-tah
                (arista)
ax.........................AH-chah
                (hacha)
bevel......................bee-SEHL
                (bisel, m)
blow torch.................soph-PLAY-tay
                (soplete (m))
bolt.......................PEHR-noh
                (perno)
   or......................tohr-NEE-yoh
                (tornillo)
bracket....................MEHN-soo-lah
                (ménsula)
   or......................soo-POHR-tay
                (suporte)
broom......................ehs-KOH-bah
                (escoba)
bucket.....................KOO-boh
                (cubo)
   or......................koo-BAY-tah
                (cubeta)
caulking iron..............kah-lah-DOHR
                (calador, m)
   or.......fee^AY-rroh day kah-lay-FAH-tay
          (fierro de calefate)
chisel.....................seen-SEEL
                (cincel, m)
   or......................ehs-KOH-ploh
                (escoplo)
clamp......................GRAH-pah
                (grapa)
   or..................ah-brah-sah-DAY-rah
                (abrazadera)
claw hammer........mahr-TEE-yoh day OO-nyah
                (martillo de uña)

```
cold chisel....................ehs-KOH-ploh
               (escoplo)
crowbar...............PAH-tah day CHEE-bah
            (pata de chiva)
drill.........................tah-LAH-droh
               (taladro)
   or.......................bah-RRAY-nah
               (barrena)
   bits..........................BROH-kahs
               (brocas)
   brace......................behr-bee-KAY
            (berbiqué, m)
   to drill..................tah-lah-DRAHR
               (taladrar)
dustpan...................ray-koh-hah-DOHR
            (recojador, m)
file..............................LEE-mah
               (lima)
flashlight..................LAHM-pah-rah
               (lámpara)
   bulb........................foh-KEE-toh
               (foquito)
funnel........................ehm-BOO-doh
               (embudo)
grappling iron......................KLOH-kay
            (cloque, m)
   or.......................sahr-HEHN-toh
            (sargento, m)
hammer........................mahr-TEE-yoh
               (martillo)
   to hammer.................mahr-tee-YAHR
               (martillar)
   or.............................klah-BAHR
               (clavar)
handle..........................MAHN-goh
               (mango)
   or.............................POO-nyoh
               (puño)
hardware...............fay-rray-tehr-EE-ah
            (ferretería)
hinge........................bee-SAH-grah
               (bisagra)
```

```
jack............................GAH-toh
              (gato)
  or......may-KAHN-nee-koh ee-DRAW-lee-koh
          (mechánico hidráulico)
knife.........................koo-CHEE-yoh
              (cuchillo)
mallet, wooden....................MAH-soh
              (mazo)
  or......mahr-TEE-yoh day kah-lah-FAH-tay
          (martillo de calafate)
marlin spike......................boo-REEL
              (buril, m)
miter box............KAH-hah day KOHR-tays
          (caja de cortes)
mop.......................trah-pay-ah-DOHR
              (trapeador, m)
nail.............................KLAH-boh
              (clavo)
  copper....................day KOH-bray
              (de cobre)
  galvanized......day gahl-bah-nee-SAH-doh
          (de galvanizado)
  to nail......................klah-BAHR
              (clavar)
nut..............................TWEHR-kah
              (tuerca, m)
oil can...................ay-say-TAY-rah
              (aceitera)
pipe..............................TOO-boh
              (tubo)
  pvc...........TOO-boh day PLAHS-tee-koh
          (tubo de plástico)
  copper.............TOO-boh day KOH-bray
              (tubo de cobre)
  cutter................kohr-tah-TOO-bohs
              (cortatubos)
  galvanized..TOO-boh gahl-bah-nee-SAH-doh
          (tubo galvanizado)
plane.........................say-PEE-yoh
              (cepillo)
pliers....................ah-lee-KAH-tays
              (alicates, m)
```

```
or........................tay-NAH-sahs
              (tenazas)
punch.........................poon-TOH
                (punto)
putty knife................ehs-PAH-too-lah
              (espátula)
saw.........................see-AY-rrah
               (sierra)
   band...........see-AY-rrah day BAHN-dah
            (sierra de banda)
   circular.......see-AY-rrah seer-koo-LAHR
            (sierra circular)
   crosscut..KOHR-tays ah-trah-bay-SAH-dohs
            (cortes atravesados)
   electric..............eh-LEHK-tree-kah
                (eléctrica)
   hack.......................say-GAY-tah
                (segueta)
   blades for,OH-hahs PAH-rah say-GAY-tahs
           (hojas para seguetas)
   hand......................say-RROO-choh
               (serrucho)
   keyhole.......say-RROO-choh day POON-tah
            (serrucho de punta)
   to saw.................say-rroo-CHAHR
               (serruchar)
scraper.....................rahs-KAY-tah
              (rasqueta)
   to scrape.............rahs-kay-tay-AHR
              (rasquetear)
screw, in Baja................chee-LEE-yoh
              (chilillo)
   wood..................ah-chee-yee-YAHR
              (achillillar)
   eye.......................ahr-MAY-yah
               (armella)
   driver...............day-sahr-mah-DOHR
              (desarmador)
   to screw.............ah-tohr-nee-YAHR
              (atornillar)
sledgehammer......................MAH-rroh
                (marro)

                   236
```

```
socket.........................DAH-doh
                (dado)
square......................ehs-KWAH-drah
                (escuadra)
tape............................SEEN-tah
                (cinta)
tape measure..SEEN-tah PAH-rah may-DEE-dahs
          (cinta para medidas)
tin snips....tee-HAY-rahs PAH-rah kohr-TAHR
   lah-MEE-nah
        (tijeras para cortar lamina)
vise.............tohr-NEE-yoh day BAHN-koh
          (tornillo de banco)
washer.....................ah-rahn-DAY-lah
                (arandela)
wrench in general.YAH-bays hay-nay-RAH-lays
          (llaves (f) generales)
   Allen................YAH-bay day AH-llen
          (llave de Allen)
   or.............YAH-bay eggs-ah-goh-NAHL
          (llave exagonal)
   box.................YAH-bay day KAH-hah
          (llave de caja)
   box end...
   .....ehs-WEETCH PAH-rah OO-nah YAH-bay
      (eswitch (m) para una llave)
   or.................YAH-bay ehs-TRAY-yah
          (llave estrella)
   crescent..............krehs-see⌃EHN-tay
          (cresciente, m)
   nut..............YAH-bay day too⌃EHR-kah
          (llave de tuerca)
   open end.......YAH-bay ehs-pah-NYOH-lah
          (llave española)
   pipe...........YAH-bay PAH-rah TOO-bohs
          (llave para tubos)
   or..................YAH-bay STEEL-sohn
          (llave Stillson)
   socket wrench........YAH-bay day DAH-doh
          (llave de dado)
```

MATERIALS

aluminum..................ah-loo-MEE-nee⌢oh
                  (aluminio)
antifouling paint.peen-TOO-rah day FOON-doh
             (pintura de fundo)
board (a).......................mah-DAY-roh
                (madero)
   or........................bah-RROH-tay
                (barrote)
brass............................lah-TOHN
                (latón, m)
bronze..........................BROHN-say
                (bronce, m)
   or..............................KOH-bray
                (cobre)
to build...................kohns-troo⌢EER
               (construir)
caulking.........kah-lay-fah-tay⌢ah-DOO-rah
          (calefateadura)
   to caulk.............kah-lay-fah-tay⌢AHR
            (calefatear)
canvas............................LOH-nah
                (lona)
cast iron.............YAY-rroh foon-DEE-doh
            (hierro fundido)
chain..........................kah-DAY-nah
                (cadena)
chrome.........................kroh-MAH-doh
                (cromado)
chromium.........................KROH-moh
                (cromo)
copper...........................KOH-bray
                (cobre, m)
cord (string)...................kohr-DOHN
                (cordón, m)
   or...........................kohr-DEHL
                (cordel, m)
cotton.......................ahl-goh-DOHN
                (algodón)
to counter sink............ah-boh-kahr-DAHR
              (abocardar)

```
or........................ehm-boo-TEER
              (embutir)
dacron........................dah-KROHN
              (dacrón)
glass........................BEE-dree‿oh
              (vidrio)
glue..........................KOH-lah
              (cola)
   or..........................gloo-TEHN
              (gluten, m)
   or....................pay-gah-MEHN-toh
              (pegamento)
iron..........................YAY-rroh
              (hierro)
lacquer........................LAY-kah
              (leca)
   or........................bahr-NEEZ
              (barniz, f)
   to lacquer..................lah-kay‿AHR
              (laquear)
lead..........................PLOH-moh
              (plomo)
leather........................KWEH-roh
              (cuero)
mahogany......................kah‿OH-bah
              (caoba)
metal........................may-TAHL
              (metal, m)
oak..........................ROH-blay
              (roble, m)
paint........................peen-TOO-rah
              (pintura)
   to paint..................peen-TAHR
              (pintar)
plastic....................PLAHS-tee-koh
              (plástico)
putty........................mah-SEE-yah
              (masilla)
rubber..........................OO-lay
              (hule)
sandpaper............pah-PEHL day LEE-hah
              (papel de lija)
```

```
to sand........................lee-HAHR
              (lijar)
to scarf....................ehn-sahm-BLAHR
              (ensamblar)
scrap iron.............YAY-rroh bee-AY-hoh
            (hierro viejo)
to shave (with a plane)........say-pee-YAHR
              (cepillar)
(a) splice.....ah-SEHR OO-nah kohs-TOO-rrah
          (hacer una costurra)
   or........................hoon-TOO-rah
              (juntura)
   to splice................kohs-too-RRAHR
              (costurrar)
spruce..........................ah-BAY-toh
              (abeto)
   or.....................PEE-noh BLAHN-koh
            (pino blanco)
steel...........................ah-SAY-roh
              (acero)
tar........................ahl-kee-TRAHN
            (alquitrán, m)
teak............................TAY-kah
              (teca)
turpentine...............tray-mehn-TEE-nah
              (trementina)
   or.......................ah-gwah-RRAHS
              (aguarraz)
to weld.......................sohl-DAHR
              (soldar)
wood..........................mah-DAY-rah
              (madera)
```

WORKMEN

```
carpenter.................kahr-pehn-TAY-roh
              (carpentero)
   ships..kahr-pehn-TAY-roh day ree-BAY-rah
          (carpentero de ribera)
caulker...................kah-lah-FAH-tay
              (calefate, m)
```

```
diver..........................BOO-soh
                    (buzo)
electrician...........ay-lehk-tree-SEES-tah
              (electricista, m)
fireman.....................bohm-BAY-roh
                 (bombero)
mechanic..................may-KAH-nee-koh
                (mecánico)
plumber.....................ploh-MAY-roh
                 (plomero)
repairman.................ray-pah-rah-DOHR
              (reparador, m)
rigger.................ah-pah-ray-hah-DOHR
              (aparejador, m)
sailmaker....fah-bree-KAHN-tay day BAY-lahs
        (fabricante (m) de velas)
    or..........................bay-LAY-roh
                 (velero)
shipbuilder...kohns-trook-TOHR day BOO-kays
        (constructor (m) de buques)
welder......................sohl-dah-DOHR
               (soldador, m)
```

Where am I?
¿DOHN-day ehs-TOY?
(¿Dónde estoy?)

If one of your nautical instruments breaks
while in Mexico, chances are you cannot
repair it until you get back to the States.
Better brush up on your celestial!

```
I need____ ...........Nay-say-SEE-toh____.
            (Necesito____.)
The course is____.....Ehl ROOM-boh ehs____.
            (El rumbo es____.)
It is your watch.
        ..........Lah GWAHR-dee-ah ehs SOO-yah.
            (La guardia es suya.)
Where am I?............¿DOHN-day ehs-TOY?
            (¿Dónde estoy?)


auto-pilot...pee-LOH-toh ow-toh-MAH-tee-koh
            (piloto automático)
azimuth......................ah-see-MOOT
            (azimut, m)
    compass.....BREW-who-lah day ah-see-MOOT
            (brújula de azimut)
    dial........................NOH-mohn
            (gnomon, m)
barometer.................bah-roh-may-TROH
            (barometró)
barometric............bah-roh-MAY-tree-koh
            (barométrico)
bearing.................oh-rehn-tah-see-OHN
            (orentación, f)
binnacle...................bee-TAH-koh-rah
            (bitácora)
binoculars............bee-nah-koo-LAH-rays
            (binaculares)
    or......................hay-MAY-lohs
            (gemelos)
callipers.......kohm-PAHS kah-lee-brah-DOHR
            (compás (m) calibrador)
chart.............KAHR-tah day mah-ray-AHR
            (carta de marear)
chronometer..............kroh-NOH-may-troh
            (cronómetro)
compass......................BREW-who-lah
            (brújula)
    card...........ROH-sah day bee-EHN-tohs
            (rosa de vientos)
    needle.......ah-GOO-hah day BREW-who-lah
            (aguja de brújula)
```

points
  east...........................EHS-tay
                (este)
    (in addresses, east is oriente,
        abbreviated Ote.)
  west........................oh⌢WEHS-tay
  (in addresses, west is poniente,
       abbreviated Pte.)
  north.......................NOHR-tay
              (norte)
  northeast.................nohr-EHS-tay
             (noreste)
  northwest.............nohr-oh⌢WEHS-tay
           (noroeste)
  south............................soor
            (sur)
  southeast.................soor-EHS-tay
            (sureste)
  southwest.............soor-oh⌢WEHS-tay
          (suroeste)

constellation........kohns-tay-lah-see⌢OHN
      (constelación, f)
course...........................ROOM-boh
          (rumbo)
dead reckoning
  ......see-too-ah-see⌢OHN day ehs-TEE-mah
     (situación de estima)
degrees..........................GRAH-dohs
       (grados)
depth sounder
  ....sohn-dah-DOHR may-KAH-nee-koh
     (sondador (m) mecánico)
deviation.................dehs-bah-see⌢OHN
      (desvación, f)
dividers........kohm-PAHS-ays day POON-tahs
    (compases (m) de puntas)
equator.......................ay-kwah-DOHR
     (ecuador, m)
fix....................see-too-ah-see⌢OHN
     (situatción, f)

Greenwich Mean Time
.......OH-rah MAY-dee‑ah day GREHN-weech
        (hora media de Greenwich)
hand-bearing compass
..ah-GOO-hah ah-see-moo-TAHL day MAH-noh
        (aguja acimutal de mano)
knot..............................NOO-doh
                (nudo)
latitude.....................lah-tee-TOOD
                (latitud, m)
longitude...................lohn-hee-TOOD
                (longitud, m)
Loran...........................loh-RAHN
                (lorán)
meridian...............may-ree-dee‑AH-noh
                (meridiano)
microphone...............mee-KROH-foh-noh
                (micrófono)
moon.............................LOO-nah
                (luna)
  full...............play-nee-LOON-ee‑oh
                (plenilunio)
  new...................LOO-nah NWAY-bah
                (luna nueva)
nautical mile..........MEE-yah mah-REE-nah
            (milla marina)
to navigate...................nah-bay-GAHR
                (navegar)
navigation............nah-bay-gah-see‑OHN
            (navegación, f)
parallels.......RAY-glahs pah-rah-LAY-lahs
            (reglas paralelas)
radar...........................rah-DAHR
                (radar)
sextant.....................seks-TAHN-tay
                (sextante, m)
sight................ohb-sehr-bah-see‑OHN
            (observación, f)
speed....................bay-loh-see-DAHD
            (velocidad, f)
speedometer............bah-loh-SEE-may-troh
            (velocímetro)

245

```
star.........................ehs-TRAY-yah
               (estrella)
sun...................................sohl
               (sol, m)
sunrise..................ahl-mah-nay-SEHR
               (almanacer, f)
sunset.................PWAYS-tah dehl sohl
               (puesta del sol)
tidal......................day mah-RAY^ah
               (de marea)
   ebb tide......mah-RAY^ah mehn-GWAHN-tays
           (marea menguantes)
   flood tide.................play^ah-MAHR
               (pleamar)
   high tide............mah-RAY^ah AHL-tah
               (marea alta)
   low tide..................bah-hah-MAHR
               (bajamar)
tide, rise and fall.............mah-RAY^ah
               (marea)
VHF........................VHF RAH-dee^oh
               (VHF radio)
walkie talkie....rah-dee^oh-tay-LAY-foh-noh
           (radioteléfono)
```

WEATHER

```
air.................................EYE-ray
               (aire, m)
atmosphere................aht-MOHS-fay-rah
               (atmósfera)
breeze...........................BREE-sah
               (brisa)
   fresh.........................FREHS-kah
               (fresca)
   gentle.........................day-BEEL
               (debíl)
   light..................MOO^ee day-BEEL
               (muy debíl)
   moderate...............moh-day-RAH-dah
               (moderada)
```

246

```
strong.......................FWEHR-tay
            (fuerte)
calm........................trahn-KEE-yoh
            (tranquillo)
choppy......................ah-DOOS-toh
            (adusto)
cloud.............................NOO-bay
            (nube, m)
cloudburst..................toor-bee-OHN
            (turbión, f)
cloudiness............nay-boo-loh-see-DAHD
            (nebulosidad)
condensation..........koh-dehn-sah-see-OHN
            (condensación, f)
doldrums
    SOH-nah day KAHL-mahs troh-pee-KAH-lays
        (zona de calmas tropicales)
drizzle.....................yoh-BEES-nah
            (llovizna)
    to drizzle..............yoh-bees-NAHR
            (lloviznar)
fog.........................nee-AY-blah
            (niebla)
    or......................nay-BLEE-nah
            (neblina)
foggy.......................broo-MOH-soh
            (brumoso)
forecast................pray-deek-see-OHN
            (predición, f)
front.......................FREHN-tay
            (frente, m)
hail........................grah-NEE-soh
            (granizo)
haze........................kah-LEE-nah
            (calina)
high pressure.........AHL-tah pray-see-OHN
            (alta presión)
    low pressure......BAH-hah pray-see-OHN
            (baja presión)
hurricane...................oo-rah-KAHN
            (huracán, m)
```

```
gale....................bee‚EHN-toh DOO-roh
                (viento duro)
gust..........................rah-FAH-gah
                (rafaga)
lightning.................ray-LAHM-pah-goh
                (relámpago)
mist..........................nay-BLEE-nah
                (neblina)
misty.........................noo-BLAH-doh
                (nublado)
moisture.......................oo-may-DAHD
                (humedad)
norther.......................nohr-TAH-doh
                (nortada)
rain..........................YOO-bee‚ah
                (lluvia)
rainbow................AHR-koh day EE-rees
                (arco iris)
rainfall
    .....YOO-bee‚ah pray-see-pee-tah-see‚OHN
        (lluvia precipitación)
squall........................choo-BAHS-koh
                (chubasco)
    or......................toor-boh-NAH-dah
                (turbonada)
storm.......................tehm-pehs-TAHD
                (tempestad, f)
stormy...................boh-rrahs-KOH-soh
                (borrascoso)
thunder.......................troo‚AY-noh
                (trueno)
thunder storm.................tohr-MEHN-tah
                (tormenta)
turbulence............toor-boo-LEHN-see‚ah
                (turbulencia)
typhoon..........................tee-FOHN
                (tifón, m)
weather.......................tee‚EHM-poh
                (tiempo)
wind..........................bee‚EHN-toh
                (viento)
```

```
windy........................behn-TOH-soh
                 (ventoso)
   It is windy.........AH-say bee-EHN-toh.
                 (Hace viento.)
```

CHARTS

```
Where is____?........¿DOHN-day ehs-TAH____?
              (¿Dónde está____?)
Look out for____.............BOOS-kay____.
              (Busque____.)
atoll...........................ah-tah-LOHN
                 (atolón, m)
bay...............................bah-EE-ah
                 (bahía)
beacon.............................FAH-roh
                 (faro, m)
   or............say-NYAL loo-mee-NOH-sah
              (señal luminosa)
bell buoy..............BOH-yah soh-NOH-rah
                 (boya sonora)
bluff.........................koh-LEE-nah
                 (colina)
breakwater.................ehs-koh-YAY-rah
                 (escollera)
brook, creek...................ah-RROH-yoh
                 (arroyo)
brow (edge of cliff).............KREHS-tah
                 (cresta)
buoy..............................BOH-yah
                 (boya)
canyon..........................KAH-nyohn
                 (cañon, m)
channel (canal)................kah-NAHL
                 (canal, m)
coast...........................KOHS-tah
                 (costa)
coral...........................koh-RAHL
                 (coral, m)
cove............................kah-LAY-tah
                 (caleta)
```

```
      or ensenada.............ehn-say-NAH-dah
               (ensenada)
current.................koh-rree‸EHN-tay
               (corriente, m)
depth..................proh-foo-nee-DAHD
               (profunidad, f)
dock............................MWAY-yay
               (muelle, m)
fathom........................BRAH-sah
               (braza)
   to fathom...................sohn-DAHR
               (sondar)
foghorn.........see-RAY-nah day nee‸AY-blah
          (sirena de niebla)
gulf..........................GOHL-foh
               (golfo)
gulley....................bah-RRAHN-kah
               (barranca)
harbor........................PWEHR-toh
               (puerto)
headland......................KAH-boh
               (cabo)
   or..........................POON-toh
               (punto)
hill......................koh-LEE-nah
               (colina)
inlet.........................KAH-lah
               (cala)
   or.....................ehn-say-NAH-dah
               (ensenada)
island........................EES-lah
               (isla)
kelp..............AHL-gahs mah-REE-nahs
          (algas marinas)
lagoon....................lah-GOO-nah
               (laguna)
lake..........................LAH-goh
               (lago)
lighthouse (searchlight type).......FAH-roh
               (faro)
   smaller lighthouse...........bah-LEE-sah
               (baliza)
```

```
marina........................DAHR-say-nah
                 (dársena)
mountains...................mohn-TAH-nyahs
                 (montañas)
mountain range................see-EH-rrah
                 (sierra)
mouth............................BOH-kah
                 (boca)
ocean.......................oh-SAY-ah-noh
                 (océano)
peak............................PEE-koh
                 (pico)
   or...........................SAY-rroh
                 (cerro)
peninsula.................pay-NEEN-soo-lah
                 (península)
piling.....................pee-loh-TAH-hay
                 (pilotaje, m)
pond.......................ehs-TAHN-kay
                 (estanque, m)
radio beacon............rah-dee-oh-FAH-roh
                 (radiofaro)
ravine.....................ohn-doh-NAH-dah
                 (hondonada)
   or.......................bah-RRAHN-kah
                 (barranca)
reef.......................ah-rray-SEE-fay
                 (arrecife, m)
river............................REE-oh
                 (río)
sand..........................ah-RAY-nah
                 (arena)
sand bar........................BAH-rrah
                 (barra)
sea...............................mahr
                 (mar, m or f)
sea coast.......................KOHS-tah
                 (costa)
sea wall.................DEE-kay day mahr
                 (dique de mar)
seashore.......................PLAH-yah
                 (playa)
```

```
shoal.........................bah-HEE‑oh
              (bajío)
   or..........................BAH-hoh
              (bajo)
spit.........................POON-tah
              (punta)
stream........................REE‑oh
              (río)
tideland....................ehs-TAY-roh
              (estero)
undercurrent
   .......koh-rree‑EHN-tay soob-mah-REE-nah
         (corriente submarina)
```

BUY A COPY FOR A FRIEND!

```
Mail check or money order for:        $8.95
            (CA residents add 6%)
        plus postage and handling      1.50
TO:
```

S. Deal & Associates
1629 Guizot St.
San Diego, CA 92107

NAME_____

Address_____

City_____

State_____Zip_____

Signature_____

INDEX

255

ABOUT THE AUTHOR:

"I never imagined when I got my degree in Spanish at the University of Kansas that I would travel extensively to Spanish-speaking countries and end up living in, of all cities, San Diego, a border town where Spanish is as common as English!" says Shirley Herd.

EASY SPANISH combines the author's ability as a teacher plus her first-hand, practical advice drawn from numerous trips to Mexico, Baja, Spain and Puerto Rico via yacht, motorhome, car and airplane.

Herd is a freelance writer specializing in the outdoor and boating fields with more than 200 published articles in major magazines and newspapers. Her first book, THE CRUISING COOK AND FIRST ADDITION, is a complete reference manual for the First Mate.

She is a member of the Outdoor Writers Association of America, the National Federation of Press Women and listed in "Who's Who in the West."